26 WORDS THAT WILL IMPROVE
THE WAY YOU DO FAMILY

/

26 Words
That Will Improve
the Way You
Do Family

DAN SEABORN

Regal

From Gospel Light
Ventura, California, U.S.A.

PUBLISHED BY REGAL BOOKS
FROM GOSPEL LIGHT
VENTURA, CALIFORNIA, U.S.A.
PRINTED IN THE U.S.A.

Regal Books is a ministry of Gospel Light, a Christian publisher dedicated to serving the local church. We believe God's vision for Gospel Light is to provide church leaders with biblical, user-friendly materials that will help them evangelize, disciple and minister to children, youth and families.

It is our prayer that this Regal book will help you discover biblical truth for your own life and help you meet the needs of others. May God richly bless you.

For a free catalog of resources from Regal Books/Gospel Light, please call your Christian supplier or contact us at 1-800-4-GOSPEL *or* www.regalbooks.com.

Originally published by Servant Publication in 2002.

Cover design by Alan Furst, Inc. Minneapolis, Minn.

Library of Congress Cataloging-in-Publication Data
(Applied for)

ISBN: 0-8307-3375-2

1 2 3 4 5 6 7 8 9 10 11 12 13 14 15 / 09 08 07 06 05 04

Rights for publishing this book in other languages are contracted by Gospel Light Worldwide, the international nonprofit ministry of Gospel Light. Gospel Light Worldwide also provides publishing and technical assistance to international publishers dedicated to producing Sunday School and Vacation Bible School curricula and books in the languages of the world. For additional information, visit www.gospellightworldwide.org; write to Gospel Light Worldwide, P.O. Box 3875, Ventura, CA 93006; or send an e-mail to info@gospellightworldwide.org.

Dedication

To my wife, Jane:
Thanks for being my dearest friend
and the joy of my life.

Alan, Joshua, Cristina, and Anna Elizabeth,
thanks for all the happiness you bring to my life.

Mom and Dad, thanks for your faithful love
and prayers over the years.

Because of all of you, I am so blessed.

Introduction

Do you ever wonder how in the world you are going to make it through the day with your family? Have you ever second-guessed God's decision to bless you with children? Do you sometimes feel you don't have the strength to do this thing called "family life"? If you can say "yes" to any of those questions, you can relate to this book.

However, if you picked up this book hoping to get answers to every family problem, then lay it back down, because it's written by a husband and father who makes his share of mistakes every day. I'm that man, and I often feel as if I've had many more failures than successes. But that is what gives me great hope in writing this book. As I talk with other parents, I feel like I am *normal* because I also see the number of struggles they face in trying to keep their families together.

These days, if you believe in the traditional family, you're going to have to fight for your family as never before. Through this book, I am committed to giving you some practical ideas and some simple words that can help you in that battle and assist you in making the changes that need to be made in your home life. I have experienced these changes myself as I have walked in relationship first with the Lord and then with my wife and children. Through these experiences, I have grown tremendously in understanding what makes a family work and how I need to daily die to self so I can live through Christ.

As you read this book, you will see many references to "the Lord" and "Christ." That's because I believe it is foundational to know the Lord Jesus Christ as your Savior in order to build a godly home. Knowing him starts with believing he died on the cross for your sins and making a conscious decision to follow him and his teachings. Every person that has made that commitment to the Lord—even though they will make many mistakes along the way—can have a tremendous impact not only on their family but also on the world.

At the end of each chapter you will find a section called Personal Moments, an opportunity to reflect on the chapter and apply it to your life. These questions are also great starters for a small group setting, with a mentor or mentoring couple leading the group. The questions are simple and allow for good interaction.

Take time to thoughtfully read through each of these chapters and reflect on the questions offered at the end. If you discover something you need to do to improve your family relationships, please follow the related suggestions. Then watch, with gratitude to God, as your family continues to grow together.

AWARENESS

There was once a married couple that had been seeing a counselor for several months. After failing to see any signs of progress, the frustrated counselor stood up, walked over to the couple, and gave the wife a big kiss right on the lips. "Your wife needs this every day!" the counselor said to her husband—who thought a moment and responded, "Well, I can get her here every day but Thursday."

It's a funny story, but it also illustrates a sad reality in many marriages—the miserable level of awareness some men have about the condition of their marriage.

A psychologist named Nathaniel Branden once said, "The first step toward change is awareness. The second step is acceptance." If you want to fix something, you've got to be aware of what needs fixing—and then, you have to accept the fact that things have to change. Two "A" words—a very appropriate way to start our journey through the alphabet together.

Like any journey, you'll get more out of this one if you know where you're going, what your goal is for your family. In our home, a recent incident provided a fitting visual image of what I want our family to look like. My wife was making peanut-butter-and-jelly sandwiches, and one accidentally fell on the floor. When it did, the sandwich stuck together.

I picked it up and said to the kids, "This is what we want our family to look like." I pulled the sandwich open a bit, but it still clung together. The jelly and peanut butter were mixed beautifully on the bread. I explained that peanut-butter-and-jelly families stick together no matter what—even when we feel as if we've been dropped on the floor.

There's biblical text that provides insight into how ours can become a peanut-butter-and-jelly family. It's found in Ephesians 5:15-20, and it offers basic principles we can follow to make sure each person in our family is aware of the needs of the others and that our family sticks together through everything we face. These are insights Paul taught to believers who had established a church in the city of Ephesus and now needed some principles for daily guidance. Like those believers, even though we have established our family on a Christian foundation, we need guidance on how to live that out on a daily basis.

In this passage, I see three strategic questions for family members. Your answers should make you more aware of the way you come across to your family.

1. Are you fun to live with?

Verses 15 and 16 say, "Be very careful, then, how you live—not as unwise but as wise, making the most of every opportunity, because the days are evil." The idea in the original Greek is to take time to observe how you live. The word "careful" in Greek is the word *akribos*, meaning "accurate and investigating." Are you willing to analyze your life so you could become more aware of how you need to live? Would you want to live with yourself? If someone in your home treated you the way you treat them, how would you react?

Jane and I once had an argument that seemed hopeless. I walked away from her and went into the kitchen where I just stood with my arms crossed. Our older son saw what was going on, popped his head into the kitchen, and asked, "What are you going to do now, Dad? Just stand there and pout?"

Jane burst into laugher. Thankfully, I did too! At that moment, I needed to make the most of this opportunity. That's difficult to do in the middle of unpleasant circumstances. But in this case, that's exactly what my family needed at that moment—and I'm glad I was aware of that.

2. Are you fun to grow with?

This passage in Ephesians also says, "Do not be foolish, but understand what the Lord's will is … be filled with the Spirit." I have discovered that following the Lord's will sets me up to be the greatest father I can possibly be. When I live the way Jesus wants me to, I am fun to grow with. When I live the way Dan wants to—usually the result of a bad attitude—I am not fun to grow with.

In a private place in my office, I keep a list of things I pray over for each family member. Next to each person's name, I've written what I believe are their top five prayer needs. For example, for one of my sons, I pray that he will

- know Christ and grow in him
- become selfless
- experience good times with Mom and Dad
- discover his spiritual gift and use it
- be patient with his siblings

There are other things on his list, but those are the top five. Here's the kicker: In order for my son to grow in these areas, I have to model this behavior for him. That is a huge responsibility, and one that I need to accept. Too many parents place expectations on their children that they themselves don't meet. Wise parents are aware that asking their children to live a certain way requires that they live in the same way.

3. Are you fun to talk to?

When I cut my wife off and finish her sentence, I know I am no fun to talk to! The same is true when I respond too quickly to my children. The best way to analyze if you are fun to talk to is to ask yourself, "Would *I* want to talk to me if I were them?"

The best talkers are great listeners. By learning to become good listeners, we become effective receivers of what others have to say. When we do speak, we need to speak to one ano-ther in a loving, caring way.

On a recent visit to an amusement park, I sat on a bench and watched as a family bickered over some stuffed animals the older son had won. The younger son was crying, and the parents were arguing. The father in particular wasn't acting much more mature than the kids were. The father and older son walked away; the mother and younger son went into a souvenir shop. From their conversation, I knew they had little money left.

Meanwhile, a man who had won a huge stuffed animal sat down next to me. I offered him five dollars for it. He pocketed my money and handed me his prize.

A few minutes later, the boy came out of the shop wearing

a little visor his mother had bought him. I called him over and asked if he liked the big stuffed animal sitting next to me. His eyes grew wide—of course, he loved it! I handed it to him. His arms could barely reach around it, but he excitedly took it and said, "Thank you, sir!"

I said, "You seem like a good kid, and I just wanted you to know that I love you."

By now the whole family was reunited. The boy's mother looked at me and acknowledged the gift. Though I could see it took some effort, the father also thanked me.

I wondered if those parents were fun to talk to, if that father was the kind I would want to grow up with. Then the question was turned on me: "Dan, don't you think you look that way sometimes? You don't always pass out the loving stuffed animals to your children. Sometimes you're guilty of yelling and frustration as well!"

It's important that we bring loving stuffed animals home to our family. Not *real* stuffed animals, but the gifts in our heart that prevent us from being judgmental and make us fun and joyful and fully aware of all that it takes to create a loving atmosphere in our family.

> **Wise parents are aware that asking their children to live a certain way requires that they live in the same way.**

Personal Moments

1. What did this chapter make me "aware" of that I need to address in my life?
2. Am I fun to live with?
3. Am I fun to grow with?
4. Am I fun to talk to?
5. How could I improve in each of these areas?

BELIEFS

We've all heard it said that if you don't stand for something, you'll fall for anything. Our society is filled with people looking for something to believe in. They're looking for leadership and a belief system they can support.

A U.S. congressman recently invited me to give the keynote address at a gathering of three hundred high school juniors who were chosen to attend a leadership summit. My speech focused on an individual's belief system. Before you seek to be a leader, I told the audience, you must define your belief system—because everything you do, every attempt you make to influence others, will be determined by that belief system.

On every grave marker I've ever seen, there's a birth date, a dash, and a death date. The birth and death dates are important, but that little dash in the middle represents the mark you've made with your life. I told the students at the leadership summit that their mark would be defined by their belief system. The question for us—especially regarding our family—is "What am I doing with my dash?"

Each day, we have the privilege of adding to that dash. Before the dash is completed, we need to define our beliefs and live them with what little dash we have left.

"I have decided that my life will honor Jesus Christ," I told the youth at the conference. "Some people will not like that, some will tolerate it, and others will celebrate it. My decision, however, must not be influenced by their opinions. Otherwise I lose my belief system."

I used a visual aid to illustrate the way we make our mark in life. Imagine that your life is making a mark, I said, one that is affected by your belief system. Which of the following marks would it be?

Fine-Point Markers

Many people make a mark so narrow that it's almost unnoticeable. *They* know what they stand for, but the rest of us have to squint to figure it out. Our families can't be little fine-point markers—our marks must be bigger than that.

Erasable Markers

These people change with the wind. Some politicians are like this: They say one thing to one group and something else to another group. As parents, we need to make sure we don't live an erasable life. We must be able to say, "This is the mark we make, and we don't change it because of the way the wind blows."

Invisible Markers

These people say they're making a mark, but no one else can even see it.

Highlighters

These people only want to be or do whatever makes them popular. There was a girl in one of the youth groups I led who was never available to go on a missions trip or rake lawns for the elderly. But if I needed someone to stand in the spotlight and sing a solo, she was *always* available. That's a highlighter—someone who is not willing to serve but wants to be noticed. Highlighters seldom make an impact; they only draw attention to themselves and live selfish lives.

Bold, Permanent Markers

This is the mark you'll want to make with your family. Believe that your family has a purpose, define that purpose, and live it out. Let your family leave a bold mark for other families to follow.

> **Believe that your family has a purpose, define that purpose, and live it out.**

After working with students for several years, Jane and I began to realize how often some families fight over insignificant things. Their belief system is flawed, because they live for things that are temporal. Arguing over nonessential issues causes children to rebel and families to break up.

To avoid that, we decided to establish what we call "Dad and Mom's Rules of the Home"—principles we are willing to die for. We believe they are essential and will help us find balance in our family life.

Please understand that these are rules we established for our home, not yours. It's important that you spend time determining your own belief system and the rules you want your family to live by.

We followed three steps in developing our rules:

1. We listened to God for guidance.

This is a discipline we have followed for years. We believe in prayer and reading the Bible, but we also believe that when you sit quietly before the Lord, he will lead and guide you. That may sound superspiritual, but it isn't.

I can't say that I have ever seen Jesus walk into the room. I can't tell you that turtledoves fly by the window every time I do this. But I can tell you I believe I have heard some things in my spirit that I needed to hear.

2. We resolved to get away together at least once a year.

Over a three- or four-day period, Jane and I spend one night discussing our family. We go to a restaurant, and after dinner we talk about our family. It was during one of these weekends that we refined our list of rules.

3. We affirmed our rules through the advice of friends and mentors.

Jane and I know several couples who have done a fantastic job in raising their children. After we came up with our list of rules, we asked our friends what principles they were willing to die for—without telling them *why* we were asking that. The answers they gave were identical to what we believe the Lord had told us.

Below are our five rules. I am not giving them for you to copy; I just want to make sure you understand the kind of principles we're talking about. Ours are posted on a placard in our house. Our kids know them and talk about them. This is essential to helping our kids understand *what* we believe and *why* we believe it.

Dad and Mom's Rules of the Home

Only positive attitudes allowed.
Bad attitudes certainly surface in our home, but they are not allowed to continue. Neither the parents nor the children are allowed to get away with having a bad attitude. That means the children are expected to have a good attitude even when Mom and Dad are correcting them.

Respect yourself and others.
When I was a little boy my mother taught me that JOY means Jesus first, Others second, and Yourself last. And if I respect and love myself, then I can respect and love others in the proper way. If you don't respect yourself, you won't respect other people.

Attend church.
This one is challenging, because I would never insist that my children attend a "dead" church. I will not ask them to go to a place that isn't growing in Christ. When I say "attend church," I mean a growing, vibrant place. Church attendance can mean youth group or a Young Life or Campus Crusade for Christ meeting. As long as they are in a place where the Lord's Word is being taught and lived out, then they are attending church.

Abide by the morals we establish.
Jane and I have a certain moral code that we live by and expect our children to live by as well. We tell our kids, "While you are in this home, you will live by this rule."

No put-downs.

Words of encouragement build character and a solid foundation for our home and for our children's future. Do we sometimes use put-downs? Of course. I use them sometimes myself, but I always apologize as soon as I realize what I've done. If our children do it, they are asked to apologize. We do not allow this type of behavior to continue.

These rules coincide with our belief system. We want to see our children grow up and follow these rules not because *we* think they are important, but because they are founded in God's Word and therefore have eternal value.

Make sure you know *why* you believe *what* you believe. Then teach those beliefs to your children.

Personal Moments

1. What are the foundational beliefs of your home? Take time to identify why you believe what you believe.
2. What are the beliefs you are willing to die for?
3. How has your childhood shaped your beliefs?
4. How are you establishing a belief system for your children?

C

CHERISH

My wife has wanted an original Amish dining room table for a long time, and we're finally getting one. We're now looking for a good home for our old table. It's in great condition considering the wear and tear it has sustained since my parents gave it to us as a wedding present many years ago. Five moves, thousands of meals, and four children later, it's still a beauty.

As a family—especially as the children have grown—we've had some serious discussions around that table. We've laughed a lot, argued a bit, and prayed for each other at that table. We've defused frustrations, balanced checking account statements, helped with homework, wiped up spilled milk, and shooed the dog off that table.

As these memories engulfed me, I began to wonder: "Why are we getting rid of this table? Too much good stuff happened here." But what's important is the people gathered around the table, not the table itself. It's Jane, Alan, Josh, Crissy, and Anna that make the table what it is. I don't need to cherish the table; I need to cherish the people.

I once knew a woman who clearly cherished her house more than she did her family. No one could touch anything in the house; everything had to be perfect all the time. It got to the point where she wouldn't let her husband in the house, because he worked in the fields and didn't meet her demands for cleanliness. I still remember the little home he had created in the garage, a place where he could watch TV and sleep. Unbelievable but true!

Let's make sure we cherish people—especially our family—and not things. A child who is cherished feels valued. A cherished spouse is a happy spouse; a cherished parent is a respected parent.

Let's look at the nuts and bolts of cherishing our family by pulling some ideas from 1 Corinthians 13.

Love is kind.

We need to treat our family with kindness and love, but frankly, being kind to our family can sometimes be tough. At work we treat people well because we don't want to lose our job. We try to make a good impression on our neighbors, and we even treat strangers with common courtesy. But at home, when we let our hair down, unkind words begin to pop out. Before that happens, ask yourself, "Am I being kind? Am I gentle and loving toward my family?"

Love is patient.

I show that I cherish my family when I am sensitive to each individual's stage of development and have patience with him or her at that level. The Greek word for patience, *makrothumein,* refers to patience with people, not with things and circumstances. To be patient means to endure the greatest frustrations and inconveniences, resisting the temptation to lash out or take revenge. It's interesting that we can be the most impatient with our family members, the people we cherish the most. Patience means that when we are wronged, we refuse to take revenge. Is there anyone in your family that is hurting from your impatience? you feel vengeful toward? Get rid of that attitude now.

Love is not self-seeking.
Recently, as I was about to leave for a speaking engagement, Jane and I paused to say a prayer for each other. I said, "I don't know if you've noticed, but I've been really edgy today."

She laughed out loud with a how-could-I-*not*-notice laugh. Then I said, "I think the reason is ..." and I listed some reasons, all of them selfish. In her prayer, Jane said, "Lord, help Dan not to be so selfish."

"What are you praying *that* for?" I asked.

"Because that's what's happening. You're being selfish."

When I try to get my own way, I'm not cherishing my family. Too many of us believe it's "my way or the highway." We have other choices: the right way, the wrong way, half way, no way, any way, and the one I would encourage you to choose, Christ's way. Because the right way *is* Christ's way.

> When I try to get my own way, I'm not cherishing my family. Too many of us believe it's "my way or the highway."

Love is not rude.

I was reading 1 Corinthians 13 one night in a hotel room, and when I got to where it says "Love is not rude," I began to feel so good about myself. I remember thinking that of all the things I am, that's one that I'm not.

Then I felt the Lord convicting me. No turtledoves hit the window or anything, but I had this sense that God wanted to show me something. He immediately reminded me of what I do when my wife comments on the way I drive. She'll say things like, "You're too close to that car!" I always give her a look that says, "What is wrong with you?" As I thought of this, I turned toward the mirror in the hotel room and made the same face; it was definitely rude! I resolved to change my behavior.

It wasn't long before my first test. Soon after I arrived back in town, we were driving down the highway and Jane pointed out how close our car was to the one in front of us. I turned to her and said, "Well, thank you!" with a great big smile and a happy face.

In disbelief, she asked, "What's the problem with you?"

"Nothing. I just wanted to thank you for pointing out that I was so close to that car."

"What's got into you?" she asked.

"I need to lose that look that's always putting you down when you remind me I'm too close to another car. So from now on, when you tell me to work on my driving, I'm just going to smile and say thank you."

She laughed, I laughed, and the kids laughed. And we talked about how much better this was than the arguments we usually had under similar circumstances.

Love keeps no record of wrongs.

The Greek word here is *logizeshthai,* which conveys the idea of an accountant using a ledger to keep tallies. The Bible says that when we cherish each other, we keep no record of wrongs. If you have a tally mark against your spouse, you need to erase it. Jesus does that for Dan Seaborn on a daily basis, and I must do that for my wife and children. Should I correct the wrongs? Absolutely. But keep a record? No.

Here are some practical tips to help you learn to cherish your family.

Refresh some of the old methods. Think about ways you cherished your family in the past and do those things again. Remember that table we discussed at the beginning? It always amazed me how a good polishing would restore its luster. That applies to marriage and family as well. We have to be committed to restoring people who need to be cherished.

Ask how. Ask your spouse what he or she needs to feel cherished. Ask your kids how you can make them feel more loved.

When Jane and I go away for a weekend, we talk about things we could do for each other. For the past few years she has said, "Cherish me more." Finally (after two years!) I asked, "What does that mean, to cherish you more?"

"It means to speak kindly to me," she said. "It means to respect my opinion. It means don't hold grudges." She could say that same thing to me year after year, but it won't happen until I take action. Today, tomorrow, next week, your action will determine when your family will feel cherished.

One final note about the table: We plan to give it away, to a family in which people cherish each other, where it will continue to provide loving memories. We want to accomplish that in our home and pass it along to another home.

Let it be your goal to cherish your family.

Personal Moments

1. What possession do you have that you greatly value or cherish? How do you take care of it?
2. What do you do to make the people in your family feel cherished?
3. Take time to let each family member share what would make them feel most cherished.
4. Consider how you feel when you are cherished. What do men like? What do women feel? Is there a difference?

DEDICATION

Every day I become more convinced that some of my contemporaries—those born after 1960—just don't get it. They don't know what it means to be dedicated to something. They lease cars, rent apartments, and time-share condos.

Only those few who have remained dedicated to something over many years have rightfully earned a reputation for commitment. To be among that small group, make sure you finish well and are dedicated in the end to what you were committed to in the beginning. I want to take you beyond saying "I do" to living "I will" by sharing with you some of the characteristics of a dedicated parent and spouse.

Temperate

Dedication is powerfully revealed in the quiet and subtle ways that we relate to family members. Being temperate is a perfect example. It means "self-restrained and not extreme in opinions and statements." My teenage son often reminds me that I struggle with this one. One of his pet peeves is my knee-jerk reaction when he tells me about a situation involving, say, a teacher. Without listening or allowing him to finish, I'll say, "I'm going to call that teacher."

"Dad, that is exactly what I didn't want," he'll respond, flailing his arms in the air. His face gets that curved look of dissatisfaction as he says, "Dad, could you just let me talk about my life without always wanting to fix it?" My impulsive responses show that I struggle with temperance. I need to be more careful with my words.

Elderly people tend to weigh their thoughts before they respond. That shows maturity and an understanding of what it means to be temperate. Would your family say you're temperate, or would they say you show little restraint when you respond?

Worthy of Respect

While it's nice to remind our spouse and children that we are dedicated to them, the *demonstration* of dedication must be more evident than the words. Your family will naturally respect you when the acts of dedication are more frequent than the words.

The same is true outside the home. Make sure you live in such a way that when people find out what you're really like, they discover you're better than they thought you were. The challenge is to live *at home* in a way that is above reproach and worthy of respect.

Mr. Darby, an elderly man, lives in a condo behind my house, and occasionally I visit with him. He'll look off toward the sky and talk about things of eternal consequence, and I find myself thinking, "Wow! I really respect this guy!" Sometimes I am hesitant to answer his questions out of fear that my responses will make me look stupid. I respect the way he thinks, and I want to make sure what I say is of value.

My dream is to live in such a way that someday my kids will say, "Dad, just give me your thoughts on this. I respect your opinion." That would be a rewarding sign of mutual dedication in a family.

> **Your family will naturally respect you when the acts of dedication are more frequent than the words.**

Sound in Faith, Love, and Endurance

One of my mentors, Jack DeWitt, is a generation older than I am. He has invested countless hours in my life over the last few years. He has shown his dedication to me, and I am indebted to him for many of the principles I now follow in running our organization, Winning At Home, and for the time he could have given elsewhere but chose to give to me.

One of the reasons I love him is because he is sound in faith, love, and endurance. I don't always like it when he points out my blind spots, but I know that his soundness in those three areas helps bring those issues to the forefront.

Find a mentor, guide, or friend who will come alongside you and counsel you in your marriage and family relationships. A wise couple or single parent seeks guidance from people who are sound in faith, love, and endurance. They can help you stay dedicated to the things that matter to you most.

Resistant to Slander and Negative Influences

A critical tongue can cast serious doubts on our dedication to loved ones. It has destroyed many a home; inappropriate comments have ruined many friendships. Knowing that, my wife and I make sure our home is free of slander. Do I laugh and joke about people? Absolutely! I laugh and joke about myself. But I never put other people down out of jealousy or a false sense of superiority. If that type of talk exists in your home, you must stop it. You cannot earn respect or mutual dedication if you are a slanderer.

Early in our marriage, Jane and I joined with a group of friends who were equally committed to overcoming this habit. Every time we said something inappropriate about someone else, we put a nickel in a jar. At the end of a month, we had enough money to pay for the expenses of a decent missions project. That steered us onto the right path, one that led us away from slander.

Another problem is negative influences. It's so easy to become addicted to things: alcohol, pornography, work, television, even food. Our society is filled with such an abundance of potential addictions that it's hard to dodge everything that's thrown our way.

If you struggle with an addiction, quote Scripture or offer a prayer to Jesus every time the addictive opportunity confronts you. And by all means, find a mentor. When you are honest and open about your addiction with another person, you will find it easier to overcome temptation. A good mentor not only will hold you accountable but also will encourage you.

Able to Teach

Recently, I came across a story about E.F. Brown, a missionary in India. He was once asked what he would most like to see in the Indian culture. He gave a one-word answer: grandmothers.

Why grandmothers? Because they so often demonstrate unconditional dedication to their loved ones. "Older women play a very important part in society," he explained. "How large a part one does not realize till one witnesses a social life from which they are almost absent.... The older women, to whom the years have brought serenity and sympathy and understanding, have a part to play in the life of the church and the community which is peculiarly their own."

I found that quote intriguing because I have great respect for what my grandmothers taught me. Their days on earth are over, but their influence and dedication will forever remain with me.

Titus 2:3-5 addresses the value of older women:

> Likewise, teach older women to be reverent in the way they live, not to be slanderers or addicted to much wine, but to teach what is good. Then they can train the younger women to love their husbands and children, to be self-controlled and pure, to be busy at home, to be kind, and to be subject to their husbands, so that no one will malign the word of God.

Paul wrote those verses to Titus, whom he had left on the island of Crete to become a mentor to a newly established church there. His mission was to help the church become dedicated to living godly principles.

That's what this chapter is about: living godly principles, for many years to come. When you do that, you become dedicated to making your family strong in God.

Not long ago, I called to tell my parents I was coming for a visit. They met me at the airport, and after retrieving my luggage, we climbed into the car. But before I turned the key in the ignition, I looked at them and said, "I want you to know why I am here. I am here because I love you, and I thank you for being dedicated to being my parents."

That was a *great* visit! It was one of the greatest visits ever, because I went there with a purpose—to thank them for their dedication.

During that trip, one evening I began playing an old hymn on a pipe organ my mother's parents had passed on to her. As we together sang the familiar words, tears flooded my eyes, reflecting years of happiness and hurt, joy and pain. My parents also began to cry, and we left the room expressing our love for each other. I don't think we will ever share that kind of time again on earth. I treasure it, because I know my parents were—and are—dedicated to loving me.

I'm grateful for parents who were dedicated to staying together and standing by me. I want to give that kind of dedication to my children.

Personal Moments

1. What are you dedicated to? How can you determine if you are genuinely dedicated to something?
2. What hinders you from being dedicated to your marriage or family?
3. Are you temperate? Worthy of respect? Sound in faith, love, and endurance? Resistant to slander? Able to teach?
4. List some ways you could be more dedicated to
   a. your marriage
   b. your children
   c. your extended family
   d. Jesus Christ

EVALUATION

If you want to improve, you have to ask yourself tough questions. Nobody likes tough questions. But wise parents and grandparents know evaluation is biblical and healthy for family relationships and individual growth.

I once spoke at a convention where the organizers evaluated each speaker in a postpresentation interview. I confess I didn't like the idea, but I learned through it. That should be your attitude as you read this chapter. You probably won't like it, but you will learn something. What follows are some principles that caring parents live by. As you read, evaluate how you are doing in these areas—perhaps on a scale of one to ten, with one being very weak and ten very strong.

Caring Parents

They talk about difficult issues.

People who are willing to discuss difficult topics in a loving way understand where other people are in their maturity.

"I do not believe there is a God," I once said to a man who had a great influence on my life. He simply replied, "Dan, I'm so glad you are willing to ask God if he really exists. It shows you're beginning to understand life and want real answers." Then, with godly wisdom, he walked me through a process of questioning that led me to my own conclusions about believing in and knowing God. I have learned to use that same method with others.

They know how to pick battles.
A young boy came home after a bad day and punched the wall in frustration, driving his fist through the drywall. He spent the next two hours trying to cover the hole, fearing what his father would do when he discovered it. As expected, the father beat the boy severely, without ever asking why he did it. Punishment was certainly warranted, but not raging child abuse.

Caring parents take the time to understand a situation and not rush into battle. Too many parents react rashly to things like unusual hairstyles and pierced body parts, creating problems and encouraging rebellion. We have too many crucial battlegrounds today; wise parents remember their own childhood and teen years and think twice before waging war over relatively minor issues.

> **Too many parents react rashly to things like unusual hairstyles and pierced body parts, creating problems and encouraging rebellion.**

They find ways to delight their families.
In *Seven Things Kids Never Forget,* Ron Rose shares the following story.

For months, an Alabama family had been looking forward to a camping trip along California's coastline. But then the father—who had a flair for surprises—said some problems had come up at work that would prevent him from going. He would be with them in spirit, he said; he knew where they would be at any given hour.

Reluctantly they drove off on their great adventure, minus Dad. That's when Dad put his surprise into action. He flew to an airport near where his family would be on a particular day. A friend picked him up and drove him to a spot on the interstate where his family would be driving. He waited on the side of the road to see the familiar station wagon. Before long he spotted the car—packed with camping equipment, eager kids, and his wife. He stepped out onto the shoulder and stuck out his thumb.

"Mom," his son yelled, "that guy looks like Dad! It is Dad!"

That father created a lasting memory. You can also make lifetime memories without going to such extreme, or expense. Consider these alternatives: A surprise visit during the day. Waking the kids for a midnight pillow fight. Calling your daughter, who now owns the business, to tell her how proud you are of her. And be sure to put "surprise my spouse at work" on your to-do list.

They let others get close to their children without being intimidated.

Generate opportunities for your children to get close to their grandparents, youth pastor, or a family friend. People you trust will affirm your beliefs. Grandparents are a great resource in this area. They and others help us step away from the edge and get a better perspective on our lives. From this new vantage point, we are more capable of effective parenting.

They build a team around their children.
Answer these questions related to your children.

    a. Emotional stability: Who is helping them learn how to laugh and cry?

    b. Financial stability: What are we doing to provide for them, both now and later?

    c. Spiritual stability: Who is teaching them biblical principles?

    d. Physical stability: Who is teaching them the discipline of the body?

    e. Mental stability: Who is giving them wisdom and understanding?

Are you pleased with the answers? If not, what steps will you take to make improvements?

They know how to let go.
One of the responsibilities of a parent is to say, "I release you."

I recently witnessed a "Christian" father reject his son because of a bad decision he made. The father removed him from his will and fired him from the family business, all in the name of Jesus. I've seen mothers try to control their adult daughters' lives and fathers withhold blessings because their children made decisions they didn't agree with. Wise parents recognize their new place in the maturing stages of their children and allow their adult children to live their own lives.

They balance sacrifice and celebration.

Sacrifice time that could be spent on other things, including yourself; personal purchases in favor of practical purchases that benefit the family; and wrong attitudes in favor of biblical attitudes.

Celebrate by saving up your money and getting away with your spouse and kids, by scheduling date nights, and by spending time together as a family.

They live by an equal justice system.

Live within the moral boundaries you establish for your children. If I teach my children that they should only watch "clean" shows and then watch a questionable movie myself, what am I teaching them? Set a standard for your own integrity and lifestyle that is even higher than what you ask of your kids.

They understand how much Jesus cares for them.

When we begin to understand how much Jesus loves us, we see how deeply we should love others. I recently found myself reading Psalm 23 as ...

A Parent's Psalm

The Lord is our shepherd, neither I nor my children shall want.

He helps us enjoy our places of plenty. He provides restful, quiet surroundings.

He guides me in paths of righteousness for his name and our kids' sake.

Although I walk through the discouraging days to the edge of death, neither I nor my children will fear, because he is with us.

His shield of protection will guard us, and his curved staff will embrace us and lift us to safety.

He prepares a table of security in the middle of an unraveling society.

He touches my soul and mind with healing, and our cup of life overflows with his joy.

Surely goodness and love will flow from me to the next generation

And I will be found faithful in the house of the Lord forever.

Parents, let's continue to care for and love our children for the cause of Christ.

Personal Moments

1. Take time to grade yourself in each of the areas discussed in this chapter.
2. What good things did your parents do that you hope to pass along to your children?
3. List two ideas that have come to you from this chapter that you can implement in your home.
4. In your home, how do you balance sacrifice and celebration?

Forgiveness

My son and I once attended a father-son event that featured a chemist who conducted several unusual experiments. There were lots of explosions that wowed the boys (and some of us dads!).

During one experiment, the chemist squeezed a drop of solution into a jar of colored water, and the water immediately changed to another color. The change was instantaneous! The chemist explained the scientific reasons for the transformation—none of which we understood, but we all nodded in agreement. The bottom line: It was awesome.

Forgiveness is like that chemical solution. It can change a person's entire countenance. But forgiveness often has to be squeezed from us for this transformation to occur. If we've been wronged, we feel justified in withholding forgiveness. However, the Lord disagrees.

Jesus spoke of this in Matthew 6:12: "Forgive us our debts, as we also have forgiven our debtors." Following his prayer are these words: "For if you forgive men when they sin against you, your heavenly Father will also forgive you. But if you do not forgive men their sins, your Father will not forgive your sins." This is as clear a statement as you'll ever find in Scripture. The Greek text suggests a definite correlation between our forgiveness of others and God's forgiveness of us. If you want God to forgive you, you must be willing to forgive others.

Let's look at this from the perspective of the family. What

would happen in our society if husbands forgave wives? Wives forgave husbands? Children forgave parents? Parents forgave children? I know ... you're already thinking of a situation that seems unforgivable. Many of us are living—rather, surviving—in situations like that right now.

My wife and I experienced two such situations, with dramatically different outcomes.

Years ago, a dispute prompted my grandmother and her sisters to part ways. I once asked my grandmother why they couldn't let the conflict go, and she said, "It's been too long, and we've gotten used to it." Wow! That's what happens. We become comfortable in our sin.

At my grandmother's funeral I wondered what her sisters were thinking as they stood by the casket. Did they wish they could do it all over again? I think so. *I* wish they had, and I'm just a grandchild. What a difference a drop of forgiveness could have made.

The second situation started with the divorce of my wife's parents. Her father left, and Jane and her five siblings—all six children under the age of ten—stayed with their mother, and her father remarried.

As with any similar situation, tensions sometimes exhibited themselves over the years.

As a couple, Jane and I prayed for direction in sharing our love for Christ with her stepmother. Then a few years ago, Anne had a heart attack. During one of my visits with her, Anne's eyes widened in fear as she described a vision she had during that near-death experience. But the experience led her to accept the Lord into her life, and she began to know the joy of a relationship with Christ.

A few months later, she was back in the hospital, and the prognosis was not good. As we entered her room, it was obvious that she was experiencing tremendous pain. Every breath seemed to be her last.

My wife knelt by her stepmother's bed. "Anne," she began, "do you remember when we would travel, all of us kids and you and Dad?" she asked. Anne nodded. I thought, *Oh no, not now!* Jane continued, "Do you remember when you would sing while we were riding? I remember thinking what a beautiful voice you had and how I would love to be able to sing like you. Thanks for sharing that beautiful voice with us. I love you, Anne."

I stood there, spellbound. Where did she get that depth of forgiveness? Anne's face wrinkled with a smile, and you could see the love and appreciation in her eyes. I knew what it took for Jane to speak those words. Everyone in that room—Anne, Jane's father, Jane and I and our children—experienced freedom in the forgiveness Jane extended to Anne.

Forgiveness doesn't always come immediately. Jane developed that ability over time and through a growing relationship with Christ.

If you aren't feeling very forgiving toward someone who has wronged you, there are steps you can take to change your attitude. The process is easy to understand, but to sift it through our complex lives and put it into daily practice is another thing.

If we are not able to forgive on our own, then we need to tap into God's supernatural forgiveness. The word "supernatural" is fitting: It is "super" in that it is above the norm, and it is "natural" in that it can come naturally to those who rely on the Holy Spirit.

> **If you aren't feeling very forgiving toward someone who has wronged you, there are steps you can take to change your attitude.**

After acknowledging our dependence on the Lord for the ability to forgive, we need to take the following steps.

Step 1: Think back to a time when someone forgave you.
Remember the peace and comfort you experienced. If you have asked the Lord to forgive your sin and save you, he has forgiven you. Spend some time meditating on this and thanking God.

Step 2: Ask God for specific guidance in your situation.
Pray for the Holy Spirit to lead you as you move toward forgiveness. Seek help from a counselor or pastor as needed. I have done this and found wonderful counsel and encouragement.

Step 3: Make a decision in your heart to forgive the person who has offended you. While sometimes it is not productive or practical to tell somebody that you forgive them, you can choose to let go of the offense and seek to heal the relationship.

Step 4: If you think reconciliation is possible, seek an opportunity to work things out with the offender. Place a call or arrange a face-to-face meeting with the person. Share your forgiveness with them. I know how difficult this is, but the inner peace that results is invaluable.

Personal Moments

1. Who is someone you, as a family, struggle to forgive? Why?
2. What are some examples of forgiveness you have seen within your family? What were the results?
3. How can you become more forgiving? What steps as described in this chapter are most difficult for you?
4. What impact has the Lord's forgiveness had on your family? How would you be different if you weren't following Christ?
5. List the names of individuals you need to forgive. What specific things could you do that relate to each step in this chapter?

Apply these principles in a role-playing scenario with your spouse or a friend to prepare yourself for the various ways a conversation could go. Spend time praying for the other party. Ask the Holy Spirit to guide you through this process.

G

GREENHOUSE

If you could choose one word or phrase that characterizes the place where you live, what would you choose? Here are some possibilities, some examples of the kinds of houses we live in:

- Igloo: As cold as ice.
- Split-level: You're on one level, and everybody else is on another.
- Teepee: Held up by a few poles.
- Brick: Sturdy but inflexible.
- Doghouse: You can't get out of the trouble you're in!

Better than all of the above is "Greenhouse," a place where productive things can happen in the family. In order to create a productive greenhouse, though, certain elements must be in place. I talked this over with several people who have built and maintained greenhouses, and I was struck by the parallels I found in the sixth chapter of Deuteronomy.

"If you want to have a productive greenhouse," one builder told me, "first you have to give it appropriate attention." Deuteronomy 6:2 tells us to teach the commands of the Lord to our children and our children's children so they "may fear the Lord your God." That involves giving appropriate attention. In a well-maintained greenhouse, plants get regular watering, feeding, and other types of care. Think of your child as a plant that needs daily nurturing in order to thrive.

The second thing about a greenhouse is this: It needs light. "If you can't find light, there is no sense in building a greenhouse," another greenhouse builder said.

Deuteronomy 6:7 says this: "Impress these truths on your children. Talk about them when you sit at home and when you walk along the road and when you lie down and when you get up." In other words, let the light of Christ shine on your family all the time. There's no sense in building a home if you're not going to let Christ come in.

God is not looking for "religious" families. He's looking for holy, righteous families that don't just talk the talk but actually live it out. We need to show the love of Christ in our home all the time.

Here are four questions to ask yourself in this regard:

In your home, what do you talk about most?
Is it you and what you are accomplishing, or how the Lord has blessed you? I don't mean that you should say the name of Jesus after every other word, but make sure he reigns supreme. Make sure your kids know that the blessings they receive come from the Lord and not from your own hands.

How do you talk most often?
Is the talk in your home characterized by anger or laughter or tears or comfort or tension? What word best reflects the conversations in your home?

Where do you talk to your kids?

We lived next door to a couple named Ben and Faye for many years. Our children often wanted to play with their children after dinner, which usually began at about 6 P.M. for both families. Our kids would call them at 7 P.M., only to be told, "We're still at our table, talking." Sometimes even at 8 P.M., Faye would say, "We're still talking."

One day I decided to find out what they were spending up to two hours talking about, so I asked Ben about his family's after-dinner conversation. "That's the time we've set aside for our children to ask anything and say anything," he said. "It's no-holds-barred stuff. It's been one of the greatest things we've done in our family." And it wasn't always pleasant. They used that time to deal with tough stuff. But they were talking with their kids.

> God is not looking for "religious" families. He's looking for holy, righteous families that don't just talk the talk but actually live it out.

Who does the talking in your home?

Fathers tend to get quiet, clam up, and avoid talking to their children. Teens often withdraw from the family, but they especially need to talk. Make sure your house is a place where everyone feels free to talk.

The third piece of advice the greenhouse builders gave was this: Watch for seen and unseen diseases.

In a greenhouse, pests and bugs are the "seen" dangers. You can spot rodents or insects, or at least the evidence that they've been there. When you do, you must get rid of them. If there are obvious pests or bugs creeping through the flowers of your family and destroying some of the beautiful leaves, you need to get rid of them. Maybe you need to act on that today.

Deuteronomy 6:10-19 describes how we sometimes take for granted those things that have been provided for us. Verse 10 says: "When you come into this land that your forefathers built, a land with large flourishing cities you did not build and houses filled with all good things you did not provide, wells you did not dig, and vineyards and olive groves you did not plant, then when you eat and are satisfied, be careful you do not forget the Lord, who brought you out of the land of Egypt."

We're blessed to have things like electricity and running water and the myriad technological advances we had nothing to do with. When people forget their blessings, they move into a dangerous area. Such forgetfulness and lack of gratitude is among the unseen diseases of our time.

Bacterial wilt is another greenhouse disease that destroys everything in its path. According to one greenhouse builder, you won't even know it's there until the damage is done.

Every family is susceptible to "unseen diseases." It's one thing to spot them in each other's lives, but it's another to be willing to talk about them. I challenge you to share with your family an unseen disease that threatens to destroy an individual or the family as a whole.

The fourth step to building a healthy greenhouse is this: Consult experienced greenhouse builders. This shows respect for those who have given us an inheritance in knowing Christ as Savior, all the way back to those faithful fathers like Abraham, Isaac, and Jacob. Deuteronomy 6:20 says: "In the future, when your son asks you ..." That's enough right there!

We need to make sure our children are still asking questions. Someday they will experience what we're experiencing now. When that time comes, what greater joy could a parent have than to see their children coming to them for advice?

Remember this: Just because you have a greenhouse, that doesn't mean your plants are healthy. Just because you've built a home with the Lord's help, that doesn't mean you're producing a beautiful family. But every family has the opportunity to grow and be healthy and vibrant. You may feel half-dead, but there's still hope. Just like a flower thirsty for water can be revived, so can your family. I challenge you to keep that hope growing as you begin to build a greenhouse and move out of the other house your family has been living in.

Personal Moments

1. What type of home best reflects yours?
   A. Igloo
   B. Split-level
   C. Teepee
   D. Doghouse
   E. Brick
   F. Greenhouse
2. In your family, where do you spend time talking together? How could you increase this time together?
3. What are some "seen" diseases that could be destroying your home from the inside? What are some unseen diseases that could be creeping up on you? How are you addressing the seen and unseen diseases?

4. Who influenced you to build a greenhouse? How do you feel about the example they set for you?

5. Based on the information in this chapter, establish three steps you can take that will help you build a greenhouse.

HONESTY

Mark Twain once said, "If you tell the truth, you don't have to remember anything." That's a great statement on one of the side benefits of honesty: People who tell the truth never have to backtrack to keep their current stories straight by trying to remember the big and little lies they've told in the past.

I learned a hard lesson about telling the truth when I was around nine years old. My friend Mike and I decided to go down to the pond near our house in South Carolina. My mother warned us not to go swimming, because for some reason she didn't want me to get my clothes wet that day. So we meandered over to a field that surrounded the pond and started throwing stones in the water. That was all we intended to do—honest. We had a major problem, though: It was one of those incredibly beautiful, warm, breezy days that just makes you itch to get into the water.

As we stood at the edge of the pond, I had a great idea. "Mike, let's go skinny-dipping!" I said. So we proceeded to take off all our clothes—sort of. That's when we unwittingly faced our second problem: At the age of nine, our notion of skinny-dipping demanded that we leave our underwear on. So we jumped into the pond and swam around for a while—and then something freaky happened. We were playing in the water near a bush at the edge of the pond when all of a sudden a snake came crawling out of the bush and right into the water toward us. You won't find his name in the *Guinness Book of World Records,* but I can assure you, Mike set the world record for the backstroke that day.

We got out of the water, grabbed our clothes, threw them on, and ran all the way home. We were absolutely scared to death! When we got to my house, my mother took one look at us and asked, "Why are your pants wet?" We were in such a hurry and we were so scared that we forgot our underwear was wet. Naturally, our pants were now wet, too.

We tried to come up with all kinds of excuses, but that didn't work. Finally, we had to tell her the truth, especially since she had just asked us point-blank, "Did you boys get in that pond?" I admitted that we had. As I recall, I paid a pretty severe price for that moment of disobedience. After Mike had gone home and my mother had punished me, I thought long and hard about what I had done. Did I wish I had obeyed? You bet I did!

I see myself in my children when they disobey me and have to suffer the consequences. I remember what it felt like to be caught in a lie and have to pay the price for it. Yes, lying is part of human nature, and we can expect our children to lie to us. But we don't have to accept it; too many parents give up and allow their children to get by with it.

Young children, usually from the ages of three to five, often go through a phase in which they tell lots of lies. It's tiring for parents to have to discipline them every time they tell a lie. But I will stand my ground and tell you that the dividends are worth it, if only you will remain faithful to insist that your young children tell the truth. If you can instill in them a high regard for the truth when they are young, then when they are teenagers and say they are at a friend's house, you will know that they really are at a friend's house.

There are a number of reasons why families struggle with honesty. Let's look at three of them.

1. It is easier to lie than to tell the truth if we think the truth might hurt.

Sometimes, we withhold the truth because we're afraid our honesty will hurt someone's feelings. But we pay a high price when we hold things in, particularly when we know we've been dishonest on some level. We don't need ulcers and all kinds of other problems that result from a disturbed conscience. We certainly don't need to "tell all," especially if it would be unkind to do so, but dishonesty is never right.

2. We are embarrassed because of what we have done.

At times, I've had to share something with Jane that I really wish I didn't have to tell her. Either it's embarrassing or I'm afraid it will hurt her feelings, so I try to avoid sharing it with her. But I have discovered that eventually, the truth will come out! I have this strong band of honesty that runs through my body. I have asked the Lord to continue to increase it, because I want to always tell the truth—to my wife, to my children, to everyone. Honesty builds strong relationships.

> Sometimes, we withhold the truth because we're afraid our honesty will hurt someone's feelings. But we pay a high price when we hold things in.

3. White lies make us think we're being honest when we're not.
The society we live in sets us up to excuse white lies. All you
have to do is read the billboards on the highway and watch the
commercials on television; easily half of them include white
lies. Sure, there is probably a grain of truth in them, but sometimes it's a pretty small grain!

Recently I snagged a great parking space in a large lot.
Problem was, it wasn't a legitimate space. I just tried to make
it into one. The groundskeeper came over to tell me to move
my car. Then he said, "Let me give you a basic standard for life;
if it looks too good to be true, it probably is!" We both
laughed, but he still made me move the car.

We often try to convince ourselves that the way we are living
as a family is fine. We attempt to squeeze our lives into "parking places" that are not appropriate. We lower the standard
and make white lies acceptable. But they're not. They're just
as illegal as the parking space I tried to claim for my car that
day.

During a test in one of my high school classes the teacher
approached my desk and asked, "Dan, are you cheating?" I
said, "No, I'm not!" Then he picked up the test, exposing the
small cheat sheet underneath. He called my bluff, and I paid
the price with an "F" that day.

I think a lot of families would probably get an "F" if they
were to be graded for their commitment to honesty. Let's
change that "F" so that it no longer stands for "Flunk" but for
"Freedom." In John 8:31-32, Jesus said, "If you hold to my
teaching, you are really my disciples. Then you will know the
truth, and the truth will set you free."

Jesus Christ focused on telling the truth. Whether he stood

before his disciples or his adversaries, he told the truth. In fact, Jesus said "I tell you the truth" dozens of times in the Bible. He is our standard, and our standard for truth should fly in the face of our white-lie society.

As we tell the truth in our home, we express our commitment to building a strong family that will honor Christ and to finding freedom through our honest exchange with each other.

Personal Moments

1. Does your family consider you an honest person? Why do you think they do? Why do you think they don't?
2. What are the particular areas of your life where you struggle with being honest?
3. How could you change any patterns of dishonesty in your life?
4. Consider ways to teach children the importance of honesty.

INDIVIDUALITY

Family should be the place where we best express who we are and develop our God-given talents on new levels. Ironically, many times it becomes the place where we are imprisoned, unable to be who we really are.

Within the family, we must recognize and celebrate the uniqueness of each other and allow the freedom for individual personalities to blossom. As we do this, we deepen our understanding of society and other people.

An intolerant attitude creates prisons around us and many times around individuals in our family. These prisons are sometimes self-inflicted and at other times family-inflicted.

Self-inflicted barriers are caused by ghosts of the past or goblins of the present. Habits, whether inherited or created, can also haunt us and hinder healthy family growth. They affect the whole family when the feelings they provoke are pent up and eventually vented on others.

Family-inflicted barriers are all too familiar in many families. Often they are created by unrealistic expectations placed on children, unreasonable demands by a marriage partner, or undesirable activities forced on family members.

So what can we do to break down these barriers? First, we need to understand that individuality does not mean freedom to do what we want. Instead, we must learn how to reach our full potential and still be a positive force within our family and our society. That should be the goal of parenting, that should be the goal of maturing children, and that should be everyone's goal.

Second, we must understand that the one person who can free us from self-inflicted or family-inflicted chains is the Lord Jesus Christ. He is the one who can help us discover our talents. As we use our talents to honor him, he gives us more.

> **Within the family, we must recognize and celebrate the uniqueness of each other and allow the freedom for individual personalities to blossom.**

In Matthew 8 we read:

When he [Christ] came down from the mountainside, large crowds followed him. A man with leprosy came and knelt before him and said, "Lord, if you are willing, you can make me clean." Jesus reached out his hand and touched the man. "I am willing," he said. "Be clean!"Immediately he was cured of his leprosy. Then Jesus said to him, "See that you don't tell anyone. But go, show yourself to the priest and offer the gift Moses commanded, as a testimony to them."

Frankly, this passage astounds me. We need to understand the destructive force of leprosy to fully comprehend Christ's great love of this man. The physical condition of lepers was terrible, but even worse was the treatment lepers received.

They were treated as if they were dead men. Lepers were banished from human society and were forced to cry out "Unclean! Unclean!" as they walked by.

Although physical leprosy has been largely eliminated, some people suffer from a kind of mental leprosy that destroys confidence, capabilities, and individuality. You can be assured there are those today who feel just as lonely and as unlovable as a leper must have felt. But in this passage we see Jesus doing three things that gave the leper hope, and they are three things we can still do today to offer hope to a family member. Here are the steps Jesus took:

1. He touched the leper.
Here is an outcast, an undesirable, an untouchable. When the leper asked Christ if he would touch him, he answered by reaching out his hand and making contact. He answered with actions before he answered verbally. That's what our family members need—someone to reach out and touch their wounded hearts.

2. He cured the leper.
Christ's touch brought instantaneous healing. Our touch doesn't bring about outward healing (though I do believe miraculous healing is possible), but we can provide inner healing every time we touch another person's life.

3. Jesus gave a prescription.
Immediately after touching and healing him, Jesus told the leper to be quiet about it and go do what was required according to

the law of Moses. I used to wonder why Jesus told the guy to be quiet. I would want to grab a microphone and tell the world. But a person who has been touched and cured needs time to recover and experience normal feelings again. Jesus knew the leper lived in the real world, and he wanted him to go through some earthly motions to set an example for others.

Our individuality doesn't give us the freedom to be who we want to be without responsibilities. The Lord expects us to manage our lives from an even greater level of wisdom.

If you have been restored and healed of a loss of your individuality, it's possible that you could use counseling as your next step to full recovery. All these steps eventually bring us to a place of freedom and renewed individuality in our lives.

Here are several steps that you might use as part of your recovery.

1. *Adjust your lifestyle.* The leper definitely experienced a lifestyle adjustment. People he had known for years weren't really sure about letting him back into their homes. Just as they had to adjust, so did he. When you change, you will need to allow time to pass before you feel comfortable in what you do and where you go.

2. *Get good counsel.* Set an appointment with a Christian counselor or pastor or friend whose opinion you value. It's helpful to talk things out and purge destructive thoughts from your mind.

3. *Find a mentor or friend to walk with you.* We have Jesus to walk with us, but a human hand and a human touch is significant on the road to recovery.

4. *Be accountable.* Tell your friend, pastor, or counselor what you're thinking and how you're coping. This might be difficult, but it's simply another lifestyle adjustment.

5. *Pray.* Nothing beats it. God will hear and answer your prayers—maybe not in your time and in your way, but you will see his hand at work in your life.

I'm sure you can think of someone in your immediate or extended family who has lost his individuality and feels like a leper. The Lord wants to use us to help bring healing. We must be willing to be used, and we must understand the importance of our own words in keeping "leprosy" at bay.

Join me. Let's cure the "leprosies" that so quickly destroy the individual joy and purpose of our loved ones.

Personal Moments

1. The opening section of this chapter identified two barriers we build that keep individuality from being expressed in the home. Do you have any self-inflicted barriers? Family-inflicted barriers?

2. What could you do to "touch" and celebrate the individuality of others in your home?

3. Think about the characteristics you observe in your family members that need to be fostered.

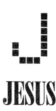

JESUS

When our daughter Anna was about three, she asked me, "Dad, who do you love the most, Mom or me?" That was quite a challenging question. I explained that I loved her and her mother equally but in different ways. We went on to the next question. "Dad," she said, with a quizzical look, "who do you love most, Jesus or me?"

I thought for a bit and said, "I love Jesus most, because if it weren't for him, I wouldn't know how to love you, and love comes from Jesus and God."

"That's good, Dad, but I want you to know that I love *you* the most."

I was about to correct her when the Holy Spirit stopped me with these words: "Dan, she is saying that because you are Jesus to her right now. You are her example of how Christ would live in your home." She needs to see someone who lives a life representative of God, and I am that person. What a responsibility—and what a reminder that I need Jesus!

"But I'm not a Christian, and I have a great marriage," someone is probably thinking. "I don't need Jesus. Our home is fine."

I am sure there are unbelieving, compatible married couples out there. But they have never experienced the depth of spiritual intimacy that comes with knowing Christ. We are spiritual beings, and without the spiritual element, we will never know that kind of spiritual closeness.

John 20 reminds us of the importance of the Lord's presence in the home. In this passage, Jesus has risen from the dead, and Mary of Magdala has just discovered the empty tomb. He appears to the disciples and says, "I am alive." But Thomas was not with them, and he had a hard time believing that they had seen Jesus. He says, "Unless I see the nail marks in his hands and put my finger where the nails were, and put my hand into his side, I will not believe it."

A week later Thomas and the disciples are together when Jesus enters the room, even though the door is locked. He says to Thomas, "Put your finger here; see my hands. Reach out your hand and put it into my side. Stop doubting and believe." Thomas responds, "My Lord and my God!"

"Because you have seen me, you have believed; blessed are those who have not seen and yet have believed," Jesus says.

Let's look at six ways in which this passage relates to our lives and helps us see the need for Jesus in the home.

We still lock doors.
We also lock our doors to Christ. Many of us have never allowed Jesus into our life because we are afraid.

We are afraid of what we'll have to give up. If we ask Christ in, we may have to change. Sometimes, holding on to what we've got—even though it causes us frustration and pain—seems easier than giving it up. Many people have never yielded their life to Christ because they are afraid of the changes that might result.

We are afraid we'll fail. Maybe you've tried spiritual stuff before and it didn't work. But if your doors are locked, you cannot experience the joy Christ wants to give you. Jesus can move into your home and give you guidance and strength, but you must unlock the doors.

Jesus still gives peace.

In John 20:21, Jesus said, "Peace be with you! As the Father has sent me, I am sending you." His disciples must have been scared when he entered that room with all the doors locked. It must have been like what we've seen on *Star Trek*. Let's be honest—every one of us would have been afraid! But Jesus came to give us peace, and he wants us to pass that peace on to those we live with.

This is where I apply what I call the "peace-piece principle." When I walk through the door of my home, I either bring in a little peace of heaven or a little piece of hell. When Christ walked into that room filled with fearful people, he brought the peace of heaven. I need to bring the peace of heaven into my family life as well.

> **Jesus can move into your home and give you guidance and strength, but you must unlock the doors.**

We need the breath of the Holy Spirit.

The defining moment is in verse 22, where it says, "He breathed on them." Our defining moment is when we allow the Holy Spirit to breathe on us. When we do that, we receive strength and power that we can't find anywhere else. For us, the idea of having someone breathe on us doesn't sound cool. But this is an inner breathing. We activate his work in our mind and spirit when we give him the freedom to live in us.

The power of the Holy Spirit helps you forgive.

Forgiveness comes in all shapes and sizes. Some of us have so much crud in our lives—little bits here and big bits there— that we find it hard to forgive those who put it there. A "big bit" for me was forgiving my father. After thirty years of a poor relationship, I didn't want to get closer to him. I had locked out the opportunity to change my attitude toward him. Then, through the help of a godly counselor, I began to forgive my father for things I had held against him for a long time. I saw it was only hurting me. We have a wonderful relationship today, because the power of the Holy Spirit helped me forgive him.

Without the Holy Spirit, we doubt.

It's worth remembering that you're human. In John 20:25, Thomas doubted Jesus was alive. Thomas needed to see the Lord for himself. The Holy Spirit had not been left on earth to reveal Christ, because Jesus had not yet ascended into heaven.

Today we have access to the Holy Spirit, yet plenty of people doubt Christ. If your home is in turmoil, believe Jesus and ask the Holy Spirit to change you and your home.

You will be blessed if you believe.

After Thomas saw Jesus and touched the place where the sword pierced his side, he said, "My Lord and my God!" In other words, "I believe!"

Jesus immediately said, "Thomas, it is good that you believe, but blessed are those who haven't seen me, and yet still believe."

That's us. We haven't seen Christ. Through the power of the Holy Spirit, we have sensed his Spirit, but we haven't seen him. If you believe in Jesus, the "J" that this whole book is about, then you too can activate the Holy Spirit, and your home life can change.

Do you want to be blessed? If you can say yes to that, then receive the gift of the Holy Spirit and believe that Christ can be the Lord of your home.

Personal Moments

1. What doors in your life do you keep locked?
2. How has Jesus made a difference in your home? What more would he like to do?
3. How could your family activate the Holy Spirit in your home?

KNOWLEDGE

A very small fraction of the knowledge needed to become an outstanding adult is found in school. Even professional teachers would admit that the most important of life's skills, behaviors, and attitudes are taught outside the classroom. In other words, if we as parents do not assume the role of teacher, we could end up with eighteen-year-old children moving from home but completely unprepared for real life—even if they earned straight A's throughout school.

I didn't learn to change a tire in school, nor did I get instruction on how to set a budget or balance a checkbook or start a business. No teacher in school showed me how to fix a leaky faucet or trim the hedges. Even though some of the better schools may teach some of these life skills, all of them will miss a big share of the vital knowledge needed for successful living.

Now here's some great news: It doesn't take special skills to be a teaching parent. Every one of us is able to impart all kinds of valuable knowledge to our children, if we are willing to bring our children alongside as we go about everyday life.

Mind you, being a teaching parent sometimes comes with a price-tag. A simple task like washing the car is no big deal—until you involve your three-year-old son in the process. You're likely to underestimate how much more time it would take or how much wetter you'll be when the task is completed. And yet, you also may forget how much fun a father and son could have with a simple bucket of soap and a high-powered squirting device. It will be time well spent, and you can figure he'll be ready sooner to add car washing to his list of family chores.

The lack of physical skills like washing the car can cause plenty of pain, but it pales in comparison to what a young adult can suffer if he lacks the kind of behavioral and spiritual knowledge that is mostly learned in the home. Even if your children are educated in a special private or Christian school, the mostly "textbook" spiritual and moral knowledge will never in itself prepare a child for successful adulthood.

Let's take a closer look at how we pass on knowledge in our families. In the Book of Psalms, chapter 78, we find a musical poem from Asaph, the chief musician of King David, which shows how we are to pass on knowledge:

O my people, hear my teaching;
    listen to the words of my mouth.
I will open my mouth in parables,
    I will utter hidden things, things
        from of old —
what we have heard and known,
    what our fathers have told us.
We will not hide them from their children;
    we will tell the next generation
the praiseworthy deeds of the Lord,
    his power, and the wonders he has done.
He decreed statues for Jacob
    and established the law in Israel,

which he commanded our forefathers
    to teach their children,
so the next generation would know them,
    even the children yet to be born,
and they in turn would tell their children.

PSALM 78:1-6

As I look at those words, I realize the importance of a father, passing on the knowledge of God to his children. This whole text teaches us that it is the father's responsibility. So, let's for a moment focus on the men and their role in passing along knowledge in their families. It goes way beyond the task of passing along a lesson or helpful information. The common saying is so true: Most knowledge is caught rather than taught. Here are several foundational truths about being a godly man in the home, and passing along godly knowledge to the next generation.

A good dad is an example of Christ in the home.
Philippians 1:27 states, "Whatever happens, conduct yourselves in a manner worthy of the gospel of Christ." I believe a man should be an example of Christ in the home, because *I know* that's the toughest place to do it. It is much easier when you're in church or at work, but taking it home is a different story. The real test of a man is what his family says about him when he's not around.

A good dad appreciates and understands personalities other than his own.

Good dads don't force their families to be like them. For example, my wife loves to sit and read a good book. She can travel into a whole different world reading that book. But I know some men who won't allow their wives to have that type of an outlet because they personally don't enjoy it. And when we as men force our children or our spouse to do the things that we enjoy and not allow them to be themselves, we do not appreciate and understand personalities other than our own. Make sure you let your kids and your wife have their own personalities and learn to celebrate them!

A good dad gives people in his home freedom to point out his blind spots.

At work we call them performance evaluations, that opportunity to get honest feedback on how we are doing. Something very similar is helpful at home. I recently pulled out a performance review I filled out in the past, and found some relevant questions for both work and home:

- Am I flexible with changes in my workload?
- Do I perform the duties assigned outside my area effectively and willingly?
- What is the overall effectiveness with my communication with the staff?

Now, let's change those three things and say it this way ...

- Am I flexible with changes at home?
- Do I perform assigned duties outside my area effectively and willingly?

- Am I overall effective at communicating with my family?

If you and I were given a job performance review as fathers, how would we do? Give it a try in your home. One way we do it is at the dinner table. I will say to the family, "How am I doing as a father? How can I do better?"

> **One of the best examples of submission is the simple act of saying "I am sorry."**

A good dad knows how to submit in all things.
I have a dear friend named Scott. We pray together on Tuesday mornings and recently, after one of our times of prayer, he said to me, "I am tired of submitting." I loved his comment because Scott is getting a little older and he is one of those gentlemen I look up to as a mentor. It isn't always fun to submit! Men have neglected to submit for many generations, and families have suffered because of it. We as men must be willing to submit, first of all to Christ, and then to our family. Submission is a radical posture that considers the needs of others before our own. When our family sees us preferring them over ourselves, they see a living demonstration of Jesus Christ.

One of the best examples of submission is the simple act of saying "I am sorry." When we have wronged a family member, those three words are a powerful outward sign of an inward submission. I do a daily radio show and my cohost, Steve Deur, recently shared on the broadcast his memory of his father coming into his bedroom, sitting on the edge of his bed and saying, "I'm sorry," and praying for him as his son. He said, "That is one of the greatest memories I have of my dad."

When we can show our children that we have the ability to say, "I'm sorry," then they have received a healthy dose of knowledge.

A good dad thinks like an eighty-year-old.

When we think like an eighty-year-old, we don't make such quick decisions, and we try to see things from all sides. I've dreamed of having the opportunity to again sit in the presence of my grandfather. In my dream, I was able to go in and visit with him and attain more of the knowledge I believe he passed on to me for many years. I woke up with such a peaceful thought. And today I can give that type of peace to my children if I will not neglect thinking with maturity and knowledge of many years.

A good dad creates an environment for healthy growth in his family.

Ephesians 6:4 says, "Fathers, do not exasperate your children; instead, bring them up in the training and instruction of the Lord." As a dad, you bring heaven or hell into your home. When you walk in the house, your children either cringe or they are excited. The option is yours. One of my favorite stories is about a little girl who had been left behind after church. Her mom and dad, by accident, hadn't picked her up, each thinking that the other parent was going to do it. After waiting a while, the pastor decided to take the little girl home. He passed down an old driveway made of dirt and rocks, and in the distance he saw her home. It was a weather-beaten old shack that really didn't look very suitable for anyone to live in. The little girl looked over at the pastor and noticed his look of surprise as he saw the old shack, and then she said, "Pastor, I know my house doesn't look very nice, but my dad makes it a great place to be from."

Dads, I don't care what your house looks like, or how much money you have. You can create a healthy environment of growth for each of your family members.

A good dad has healthy self-esteem.
This one is huge. In order to have self-esteem, you must have three things: (1) you must understand your purpose; (2) you must appreciate your talents; (3) you must know the source of your value.

I've sought to operate my life under the pie principle. Of all the things that the "pie" of life includes, I've devoted my life to making a mark in the pie slice called *family*. When I understand that my sliver of the pie is focused on family issues, it gives me an identity that builds my self-esteem.

Most of all, true self-esteem is found when we find our identity in Christ, when we appreciate the value that he places on us. Find your value in him, and your family will do the same. Your children will sense the health of your self-esteem, and they will develop healthy self-esteems as well.

A good dad knows how to communicate with his family.
If we do everything else, but we neglect to talk to our family members, we've missed an incredible opportunity to shape

their lives. Our children need our words of encouragement. They need to hear us speak kind words about their mother.

Talk to your children about their relationships with others in the family. Help them understand what it is like to deal with people outside the family. This kind of relational instruction is a major contribution of knowledge that will be useful throughout life.

Obviously, these things aren't only applicable to dads, but to everyone in the family. Let these practical ideas give you some new ways to grow in knowledge and maturity in your home.

Personal Moments

1. What are some of the nuggets of knowledge that have been passed on to you from your family of origin?
2. What are you doing to pass knowledge to your children?
3. Rate yourself in the following areas (10 is high, 1 is low):
   - Am I a good example of Christ in the home?
   - Do I appreciate and understand personalities other than my own?
   - Do I give people in my home freedom to point out my blind spots?
   - Do I seek to submit in all things?
   - Do I think maturely?
   - Do I create a healthy environment for family growth?

LISTEN

You probably figured *listen* would be the "L" word. We hear it from psychologists, from pastors, from our spouse, from our children, even from radio hosts: "Listen, listen, listen!" Ten years ago, I discovered something amazing about listening, and ever since, I have learned one lesson after another about the art of listening. In that time, I have worked on my own listening skills so I could understand the needs of my family and discern the will of God.

The story begins in the early 1990s, when I met a former missionary to India named Mary Geegh. Mary had written a small, forty-page book called *God Guides,* and its impact on my life ranks right after the Bible. I discovered that she was living in a nearby nursing home, so I paid her a visit. She was in her nineties at the time, and though she was weak and frail, her mind was as sharp as ever.

I asked her about the incredible stories she told in her book, stories of times God had spoken so specifically and clearly to her that it seemed nothing short of miraculous. I asked if the incidents she described had really happened.

She looked at me, and in her aged wisdom asked, "Dan, have you ever tried it?"

"Tried what?"

"Tried listening."

"Mary, I don't know how." It was embarrassing to confess

that, because I had spent ten years working and praying with teens and families, doing what I considered to be ministry. Yet I had not really learned to listen to God. I knew all the right verses, like John 10:27 ("My sheep listen to my voice; I know them and they follow me. I give them eternal life, and they shall never perish; no one can snatch out of my hand") and James 1:22 ("Do not merely listen to the word, and so deceive yourselves. Do what it says"). Yet after my visit with Mary, I knew I had a long way to go in developing the art of listening to God.

It isn't that easy. But there are some principles that have helped me over the years and will in turn help you get started. I've had the privilege of teaching them to families, parents, grandparents, corporate leaders, and others, and it's been a joy to see their lives changed as a result. Here are some of the "hows, whats, and wheres" of learning to listen to God.

How to Listen to God

Get alone with him.

I don't know about you, but I find myself getting busier and busier all the time, despite our many "time-saving" technologies. Unless I discipline myself to get alone with God, he always gets edged out.

You may ask, "How do I get past all my busyness? How can I change things so I can be alone with God?" Well, you just do it. Discipline is never easy. I get up at 5 A.M. every Tuesday and spend an hour alone with the Lord. On other days, I try to have a brief time of listening to him as well. But I've discovered that I have to get alone with him if I expect to hear him.

Stop talking.

Most of us talk to God when we do manage to spend time with him. We pray and bring problems to him, and that's great. But if you want to develop the ability to listen to him, you've got to be quiet. Likewise, we can talk all day to our children, but if we want to know what they are thinking, we have to close our mouth and let them open theirs.

What to Expect When You Listen to God

Expect stuff to crowd your mind.

I could hardly believe what happened the first few times I got alone with the Lord to listen to him; things came to my mind that I had long forgotten about—things I didn't want to remember, things I had often wondered about. I quickly began to write everything down so I wouldn't forget it. I do believe that Satan loves to distract us from the presence of God, but I also believe we seldom quiet our minds long enough to really think and remember important things. Expect the long-forgotten to resurface as you try to get alone with God.

Expect distractions.

First I heard a bird chirping, then a faucet dripping, and finally a lawn mower humming in the background. Anything and everything will distract you! Sometimes, the most distracting thing is the dead silence. We so rarely hear silence that it can be overwhelming when we are in its presence.

Expect revelation.

When I first began to listen to God, I absolutely dreaded my time with him because it seemed he was always pointing out something else I needed to confess or a different way I could improve my marriage and my family life. If you aren't ready to grow, if you aren't ready to improve, if you aren't ready to be challenged, you're probably not ready to get alone with God.

Expect guidance.

For me, this has been the most joyful and rewarding part of listening to God. I've sensed his direction in many ways, and I've been thrilled to respond and do things that sometimes seemed silly. But they were what the Lord wanted me to do.

> **If you aren't ready to grow, if you aren't ready to improve, if you aren't ready to be challenged, you're probably not ready to get alone with God.**

Where to Go With What You Hear

This is the million-dollar question. I've heard lots of people say, "God spoke to me" or "God told me to ..." Sometimes, I'm not sure we're listening to the same God. Often, the people who best know how to listen to God are the quietest about what they hear.

When God speaks to me and gives me direction, he does so personally. I sense that I am to share that direction with my wife and maybe one or two mentors, but then I need to internalize it and keep it to myself.

So often, people who go around talking about what God spoke to them are really glorifying themselves by trying to make themselves appear to be more spiritual than other people. By contrast, those who have developed the art of listening to God are generally humble and quietly submissive to his will.

Here are some things you need to do once you hear from him.

Go do God's will.

Mary Geegh's book was a simple book about obedience and humility. When you listen to the voice of the Lord, you will always be humbled. You can be certain you are hearing his voice if what he says places his agenda first, before your possible selfish desires. Here's a test: Is this thing I am hearing about me or is it about God? Great question!

Go to prayer.

Take what you hear from God and pray that he will confirm it through your spouse, through your mentors, through others in your life who have no idea what you've heard from him—even through your children.

Go to your spiritual mentors.

I love to run ideas by my mentors in the faith; they challenge me and keep me on track. My spiritual mentors are those who over the years have developed an extraordinary ability to sense God's direction. When I'm their age, I pray that I will have matured in my faith in such a way that my family and friends will consider my advice to be godly.

It's the truth; listening truly is an art. It's a gift from God to be able to quietly sit in his presence and receive his wisdom and guidance. If you want to grow, if you want to get closer to your family, if you want to grow closer to God, work on developing the art of listening.

Personal Moments

1. What kind of listener are you? With regard to God? To your family?
2. What would it take for you to become a better listener?
3. As a family, discuss ways you could better listen to each other. Discuss the how-to's and the where-to's.
4. As a family, discuss the idea of listening to God. What does that mean to you? Why would you want to listen to him?

MODELING

The debate continues: Just who *is* a role model? I believe every adult should be a role model, especially parents.

Several years ago NBA player Charles Barkley said he was not a role model but that parents are. Well, he's wrong, and he's right. He is right in saying that parents are supposed to be role models, but he's wrong in denying that he's one himself. Adults that have influence over children are responsible for the way they model their behavior. The question then becomes, "What are we supposed to model?"

I've found answers to that question in unlikely places, including a fitness club that my wife and I once joined. During one of our first visits, I noticed a sign that read, "The Ten Most Common Mistakes Made by People in the Gym." As I read it, I realized the principles on the list were also valid for parents. Based on that list, here are ten principles for parenting that will help you become a great role model.

1. Properly stretch before parenting.

In the gym, stretching makes a body flexible, and ultimately prevents injury. As parents, to "properly stretch" involves remembering your own childhood before you point the finger at your children. Before you correct your children's behavior, try to remember three things: what, who, and why. Remember *what* you were like when you were their age. Remember *who* they are, with their distinct personalities. Remember *why* you are doing what you are doing. Are your actions built on a solid moral foundation? If not, you'll be all over the map trying to explain your reasons to your children.

Ten years ago, a mother and father called me and expressed frustration with their daughter, who had broken one of their rules: She had eaten a piece of candy. This had become a huge issue. I disagreed with their reaction to their daughter's disobedience, but they defiantly stood their ground. I remember telling my wife to never let me be that unreasonable with our kids.

We certainly need to instill the importance of obedience in our children. But to go crazy because they have a piece of candy is a bit extreme, especially when we remember what we were like as kids.

> It helps to remember that parenting never goes away. We'll do it until our grave day. Try to relax in the process. If we take one stage too seriously, we will burn out and won't have the strength to continue.

2. Know the rules and live by them.

If everybody keeps the rules in a health club, all the members are safer and happier. It's important for parents to establish moral guidelines for the home and adhere to them. We cannot give ourselves license to break the very rules we've told our children to follow.

3. Have cool-down periods.

It's common to see people skip their cool-down after a workout, not realizing how important it is for overall fitness. While cooling down may seem like a waste of time, it is just as important as the strenuous exercise—and the same is true in parenting. All parents—especially at-home moms—need time to get away. Our children know that when I announce "Mom and Dad time," we need a break. We've spent time with them, we've played with them, we've talked with them, and we've done stuff with them all day. Now it's *our* time, and that's important. It lets our children know we genuinely enjoy each other. This is a great example for children to follow as adults.

4. Remember that parenting is a process.

Some newcomers to a fitness regimen get frustrated when they don't see instant results. We parents can also feel the same when our actions toward our children don't seem to be paying off right away.

It helps to remember that parenting never goes away. We'll do it until our grave day. Try to relax in the process. If we take one stage too seriously, we will burn out and won't have the strength to continue. If we establish a strong foundation, remain faithful through the years, and finish strong, our children will look to us as role models.

5. Pour refreshments into your mind.

A person who is working out needs to pour powerful fluids into his or her body for restoration and strength. In a similar way, parents need to rejuvenate and strengthen their minds as well. The Bible tells us in Proverbs 24, "By wisdom a house is built, and by understanding it is established." We acquire that wisdom from God's Word. As you pour his refreshing thoughts into your mind, you will have the strength to continue this thing called parenting.

6. Effective parents will get weary.

While some workouts leave us feeling energized and productive, other days we just feel like collapsing back into bed—and that's normal. It's OK to feel dead tired every now and then and want to give up. Effective parents will be tired and weary. But our day of celebration is coming.

Recently, I sat across the table from an older couple at a wedding ceremony. Bill and Paula are grandparents. "You know, the kids are out of the home now," Bill said. "My wife and I are able to travel a bit. This is the greatest time of my life. If I could pause my life right now, I would. This is it."

He's paid his dues, but his work paid off, and now he is able to influence his children and finish strong because he has been faithful through the years.

7. Handle your children with care.

Any fitness trainer will push a body toward greater achievement, but only with gentleness and understanding of physical limitations.

A body must be handled with care, and the same goes for children. If you take a ball of yarn in your hand, hold the loose end, and drop the rest on the floor, you have a vivid illustration of how to handle your children with care. Many parents yank at the end of the string, trying to get the ball of yarn to come back up—when all they have to do is bend over and pick it up to keep the yarn from unraveling. Parents who don't handle their children with care unravel not only their lives but also their children's lives.

Today, wherever your kids are, however old they are, reach out and pick them up. Roll them up in your hands, roll the yarn back onto their life, and handle them with care.

8. Teach responsibility.

Our health club reminded us that to act responsibly keeps everybody safer and happier. We do well to teach responsibility to our children—after we demonstrate it ourselves.

When I was young, one of my favorite TV programs was "The Andy Griffith Show." In one episode, Opie had thrown a rock through a window, and Andy, Opie's father and the town sheriff, made him pay for the window. A man in one of the jail cells witnessed Andy's handling of the situation and said, "I can't believe you'd make your son pay for that window." Andy turned the tables on the man, pointing out that if the law-breaker's father had made him take responsibility for his actions, he might not have ended up in jail.

Do you bail your children out? Do you admit that your child makes mistakes? Do you hold him responsible for those mistakes? We need to teach our children to accept responsibility.

9. Build a mentor into their lives.

There's nothing like a good trainer to improve our results in the gym. At home, our children look to their parents as the primary trainers, but they also can benefit from having other mentors as well. Some parents feel threatened when their children establish friendships with other adults. Nearly all children will do this, and you would be wise to direct them toward people with whom they can have healthy friendships. If we do this for our children, they will see the importance of having mentors and will establish mentors for our grandchildren.

10. Enjoy yourself and pray for yourself.
If working out in the health club is drudgery, there's very little chance you'll maintain your healthy routine. The same is true in parenting, and I believe that prayer helps us keep the joy and fun in parenting. We can turn our parenting problems over to a God who is much more powerful and capable than we, and then we can relax and enjoy the ride.

I daily ask the Lord to bless me as a father and as a husband. I can't do this stuff without God's help. I encourage you to pray that the Lord will help you be a godly model for your children and that they will follow the example you have established.

These simple, practical tools will be great modeling steps for your life and also for your children. Remember, more is caught than taught. Let your life's actions be the example your children will follow.

Personal Moments

1. Who are the role models for your family? Your children? Who are the people you most admire and would love to emulate?
2. How are you doing with the ten specific things listed in this chapter?
3. Who are the people you know that could be your mentors? How can you develop relationships with them?

NOURISH

In Matthew 5, we find one of the best-known sermons of Jesus, the Sermon on the Mount. In it, Jesus sums up many of his teachings. He begins the sermon with what we call the Beatitudes, which simply means "perfect happiness."

As I thought about the first part of his sermon, I began wondering what it would take to create perfect happiness in our homes. I believe it comes down to the value of the nourishment we offer our families, the spiritual and emotional and relational "food" that nourishes the soul.

In the following section, I've taken the Sermon on the Mount and extracted principles from it that show us how we as parents might become better at offering quality nourishment to our children and to each other.

A nourished family places its trust in God.
In Matthew 5:3, Jesus says, "Blessed are the poor in spirit, for theirs is the kingdom of heaven." I had always thought "poor in spirit" referred to someone who is down and discouraged, but the original Greek suggests the idea of a person who has nothing at all. I can assure you, when our families feel they have reached this point, we must put our whole trust in God. To do that we need to be completely detached from things and completely attached to God.

I came to understand this passage in a whole new way when

I had to take Jane to the hospital for some unknown problem, possibly appendicitis. As I waited in the emergency room while she underwent a number of diagnostic procedures, I suddenly realized there was absolutely nothing I could do to control or even help the situation.

All around me, emergency room personnel were scrambling to care for the incoming patients—this one with a heart attack; that one, a tiny baby, teetering on the brink of life and death. "This is the place where I am poorest in spirit," I thought. "I can do nothing at all." I knew I had to fully entrust my wife, my family, and myself into the care of God. That wasn't easy to do, until later when I heard Jane was going to be fine. Life holds moments like that for each of us, moments when we are so poor in spirit, so powerless, and so needy that we have nothing but our faith in a faithful God.

A nourished family exhibits self-control.
In Matthew 5:5, Jesus says, "Blessed are the meek, for they will inherit the earth." Most of us tend to think of meek people as shy and timid, but the word refers to people who demonstrate humility through self-control. When we are self-controlled, our impulses are in check, our passions are correctly focused, and our life is marked by discipline. It's a great testimony to a family to see each member—father, mother, teenagers, and even the younger children—exhibiting self-control.

Holly is a young woman with a disability that causes her to lose her balance. Recently she got help in the form of a beautiful black Lab named Delcie. Delcie underwent many years of training before he could be useful to Holly, who now holds on to a brace attached to Delcie's chest so she can maintain her balance. As for Delcie, he's practically a poster dog for self-control. Holly has the confidence of knowing that Delcie will never veer off course, chasing after cats or pulling her down an alley so he can sniff the garbage or stopping at a fire hydrant to do what dogs do at fire hydrants.

I want to be like Delcie, a self-controlled, stabilizing force for my family. I want my children to be able to hold on to me, knowing I won't veer off course. I want to be so disciplined that I nourish them by the way I walk and the way I guide them.

A nourished family goes after God as a thirsty man goes after water.

Verse 6 reads, "Blessed are those who hunger and thirst for righteousness." A family that seeks God above all else is a family that will find its fill in the things of God.

I once went snorkeling with my son out on the Great Barrier Reef off the coast of Australia, an area replete with multicolored fish, multicolored coral, and astounding ocean views. After several hours in the hot sun and salty water, we were both very thirsty. There we were in that huge ocean, but we were unable to get a drink! It reminded me of what the cohost on our radio show, "Family Stuff," once said: "The world offers an ocean of unsatisfying water!" The advertising world in particular promises so much and delivers so little that's satisfying. It's like taking in a mouthful of salty water when your throat is parched—it may look like the real thing, but it doesn't do the job.

The bottom line is this: God is the one who satisfies us by quenching our spiritual and emotional thirst. And the thirst-quencher he offers is as refreshing as clear, icy water from a mountain stream.

A nourished family is kept free of sin.
Verse 8 of Matthew 5 says, "Blessed are the pure in heart, for they will see God." Pure in heart means "rid of all sin." William Barclay, the great Bible commentator, gives us a beautiful illustration of this concept: He says it's like shucking an ear of corn and cleaning off all the little stringy hairs lodged between the kernels. My mother used to use a corn brush to get rid of those hairs; she'd brush row after row to make sure they were all gone. My own children don't like corn on the cob because of the hairs that get stuck in their teeth.

We're usually pretty good at shucking off the big sins—if nothing else, they're easier to see—but we need to remember to get rid of all the little hairs of sin that get caught in our family and threaten to contaminate it.

A nourished home is filled with peace.
Of all the Beatitudes, the one expressed in Matthew 5:9 is to me the most beautiful: "Blessed are the peacemakers, for they will be called sons of God." Most homes are destroyed by civil war—either the good-versus-evil war waged in the life of one family member, or a war that pits one family member against another. Think about it: Civil war of one type or the other causes couples to divorce, leaves children feeling unloved, and creates untold heartache as family members go at each other.

In our family, I'm the cause of conflict about 90 percent of the time. I don't like to admit that, but it's true—and I have to be willing to face that fact and then get help. I cannot nourish my family and bring peace to my home if I'm the one causing turmoil. Thankfully, the number of battles I start is decreasing, but I'm trusting God to bring me to a point where I'm free and clear of my conflict-causing tendencies.

A nourished family stands for Christ—no matter what.
If your neighbors think you are naïve in your commitment to living a moral life, I want you to know that you're OK! If your coworkers think you're foolish and intolerant because you believe in Jesus, I also want you to know that you're OK!

If we want to nourish our family, we have to be willing to be publicly identified with Christ. That's going to make us unpopular at times, and misunderstood more often than not. It means that people will get us confused with well-known Christian leaders who have blown it, and we'll be branded because of their sin. We may be laughed at, demeaned, and humiliated. Kids need to be prepared for the kind of abuse they may face, and they need to decide ahead of time that they will stand for Christ, no matter what. And as parents, we need to make that same decision.

> **If we want to nourish our family, we have to be willing to be publicly identified with Christ. That's going to make us unpopular at times.**

High-quality nutrients help make our bodies physically strong. High-quality spiritual nourishment gives us the strength to withstand the attacks and the persecution and the ridicule that may come against us when we publicly identify ourselves with Christ.

There you have it—six ways you can begin to nourish your family. As you read other portions of the Bible, you'll no doubt find more. Throw out the junk food, the wisdom of the world, and replace it with the nutrients your family needs to grow together, healthy and strong.

Personal Moments

1. What are the ways you nourish each other in your family?
2. Based on the six points of this chapter, how are you doing with
    a. Placing your trust in God?
    b. Exhibiting self-control?
    c. Going after God?
    d. Keeping free of sin?
    e. Being filled with peace?
    f. Standing for Christ?

    It will be helpful to establish how each family member is doing in these areas. Not to attack and discourage, but rather to pray for growth in these critical areas.
3. Spend time in prayer for growth in these areas.

OBEDIENCE

I learned obedience as a child by putting away my toys, by cleaning my room, and when I got a bit older, by mowing the lawn when Mom asked me to. However, the true test of living a life of obedience came in the summer of 1994. By then, I was married and had a successful career in finance.

Jane was a high school algebra teacher, and that summer she had volunteered to serve as a counselor at our church youth camp for a week. All that week, when my workday was done, I would drive to the camp two hours away to be with her and attend the evening services. During one of those services, as I stood along the back wall listening to the speaker, I sensed the Lord speak very clearly to me. He asked me, "Will you give up your career and pursue me fully and dedicate your life to ministry?" Huh? How could I do that?

That night, I did not tell Jane what had happened during the service. As I drove home, my heart and my thoughts were racing. For two days I considered what the Lord had said, prayed about it, waffled back and forth, and finally decided I would be obedient. Obedience, in this case, meant life change, career change, relocation, more schooling, and plenty of sacrifice. We had just bought a new house and a new car. But I knew I had to obey. I asked the Lord for only one thing—Jane's affirmation.

On the final night of camp, I picked Jane up to drive her

home. On the way back, I asked her if she would be willing to sell the house and car. Her immediate reply was, "If it's because you feel called to go into ministry, let's do it." I was blown away! I told her about the experience I'd had during the service earlier in the week. Right then and there, we both committed ourselves to a life of obedience to God's will.

That commitment has endured. We've moved and obeyed and died to self and obeyed and sacrificed and obeyed. We've discovered that a life of obedience is a tremendously challenging and joyful one. I'm convinced that the kind of obedience our parents instilled in us when we were young prepared us for the life of obedience we've tried to live for Christ.

> ## When I show my children unconditional love, obedience is a natural response.

There's a passage in the Bible that underscores the importance of learning to obey. In the book of John, chapter 14, Jesus says in verse 23, "If anyone loves me, they will obey me." It's a simple verse, but it packs a powerful punch. It implies that we must have a love commitment to the Lord in order to obey him. If you aren't committed to a loving relationship with Christ, you certainly will not be willing to obey his commands. That same principle holds true in our family relationships. If there is no love-based commitment to each other within our family, there will be no desire to obey.

The reason my children are willing to obey me is because

they have seen the commitment of my love to them. When I show my children unconditional love, obedience is a natural response. When the Lord expresses his unconditional love to us—and we recognize it—then obeying him is the most natural response in the world.

We need to make sure we are teaching the principle of love-based commitment within our family. As we earn our children's respect through that commitment, obedience should be a natural outflow of their lives.

But no matter how strong your commitment to your children is, no matter how loving your family relationships are, there's no doubt about it—trying to teach children to obey is a tiring and mundane and seemingly never-ending job. It takes time and effort to earn their respect, at their various levels of maturity, before obedience begins to flow.

I recently had the privilege of speaking to a group of NASCAR drivers, crew members, and their spouses. One couple told me they were tired of teaching their children obedience, "day after day after day." I applauded them and said, "Good for you! I love to hear that you are being faithful to teach obedience. It is tiring, but it is rewarding!" All the parents there expressed relief when they realized that teaching obedience isn't easy and that it takes work and effort. They apparently thought it should be easier, that they were doing something wrong. They left that day with a far different understanding of the task they faced at home.

Here are five points to keep in mind as you grapple with the task of teaching your children to obey:

1. Understand *why* you need to teach your children to obey.
It isn't so you can lord it over them; there are lifelong principles involved, and they have a direct bearing on your children's relationship with God.

2. Be persistent.
Don't give up! It's not a choice—you must persevere.

3. Be prepared for protest.
You're likely to hear some variation of this: "Nobody else has to do this kind of stuff!" Kids have a knack for finding other kids whose parents don't require the same level of obedience that you do. (They also know parents who are more demanding, but you won't hear about those people!) Expect those comments, and simply dismiss them. They're designed to distract you, but stay focused on your commitment to rearing obedient children.

4. Balance love with obedience.
The key word here is "balance." If parents aren't careful, they can become so possessed with forcing obedience on their children they forget the importance of teaching in love. The result can be very rebellious children who reject any form of guidance or rules.

5. Make sure your lifestyle is one that is steeped in obedience to the Lord.
As your relationship with the Lord continues to deepen, you will become more and more sensitive to the Holy Spirit. As you do, you will experience more and more opportunities to

obey—and to obey immediately. As your children witness this, you are offering them a picture of what day-to-day, or even minute-to-minute, obedience to God looks like, a picture they can carry with them into adulthood.

Personal Moments

1. In what ways did your parents teach you obedience as a child? What did they do right or wrong?
2. How have you parented your own children differently? What have you done right or wrong?
3. How has your obedience to God been an example to your children? How could you be more obedient to God?
4. Establish some steps to help you overcome the frustrations that come with teaching your children to be obedient.

PRAISE

Jesus said in Matthew 21:13, "My house will be called a house of prayer." Let me offer this variation to use in our homes: "My house will be called a house of praise." Too few families know what it is to praise the Lord and to praise each other. Let's look at several types of praise that need to be alive in our homes.

Praise to God

Our Father, our Creator, deserves our praise. We could not do anything if God didn't allow us to. I believe many people think this, but few translate the awareness of this truth into a reality in their lives. Prayer only comes to the forefront of society when there's been a terrible tragedy, but soon the emphasis on calling on God dissipates. But we must maintain a consistent emphasis on prayer within our family.

One of the things I enjoy is pick-up basketball games. I recall going to a nearby city park one time and waiting my turn to get in there and throw some elbows with the streetball players. I finally got in the game and soon found myself frustrated by the language some of the guys were using. One particularly talented athlete always took God's name in vain when he missed a shot. I finally had all I could take and went up to him and knocked the ball out of his hands. I held it and looked at him. He looked down, way down, and glared at me.

"What are you doing?" he yelled. I calmly said, "You know, God has given you a great ability to play basketball, but I don't understand why you damn him every time you make a bad shot. Why don't you start praising him and not putting him down?"

At first he just stood there, but I could tell he was thinking about what I had said. Finally he said, "I'll try." It was the best defense I'd ever put on anybody; he was so focused on saying the right thing that his game fell apart.

After the game he said, "I didn't like what you did, but you do have a point." And I think that's the point everybody is missing. God made us, and he made us to praise him. We need to emphasize this teaching in the home.

Praise to Jesus Christ

Our salvation hinges on the Lord Jesus Christ. He deserves our praise.

The Scriptures teach us that the Lord inhabits the praises of his people (Psalm 22:3). In other words, if we praise him, he will be with us. If we have a home where parents and children praise the Lord, then the Lord's presence will be in our home.

One of our daughters recently asked, "Why does Jesus want us to praise him? Isn't that kind of focusing on yourself?" I thought this was a great question, since we teach our children to let *others* praise them and not to seek praise. We need to see that Jesus wants us to praise him because our praise exalts the Father in heaven. Christ asked for our praise only because he was willing to completely give himself for us first.

Let's put that in a family context. Mothers are typically the servants in the home. They work to provide food and nice clothes and loving care for everyone in the family. It's very easy to praise moms because of what they do for us. That same principle is true for Christ. He has provided hope and life and salvation and care for each of us. It is therefore natural to praise him. We must remember the importance of teaching every family member what Christ has done for them. One of the results will be a desire to praise him.

Praise to the Holy Spirit
The Holy Spirit is the power of the Lord that lives within us. The Holy Spirit deserves our praise. John 13:15 gives us a glimpse of the Lord's desire to do all he can to help us with our family life: "I have set you an example that you should do as I have done for you." When the Lord rose again and left the earth for heaven, he promised that "the Counselor" would come and provide daily guidance for us. When your family experiences joy, the Holy Spirit is there; when your family experiences pain, the Holy Spirit also is there.

The Greek word for counselor is *paracletos*, which refers to something similar to a defense attorney, an advocate. I studied this word intensively to discover its practical application in our lives. As I prayed for insight I kept thinking the word *paracletos* ... *paracletos* ... *paracletos* ...

As I said the word over and over in my mind I began to think of the phrase "pair of cleats." My children play baseball and soccer, and they use cleats every time they play. It occurred to me that relying on the Holy Spirit is like wearing a pair of cleats. Cleats give added traction and keep us from slipping on the soggy soil. You get better starts and stops with cleats. They are designed to give you grip! And getting a grip is critical to being the example we need to be in our homes.

> Point out each other's good qualities. Have "praise wars" and compliment the socks off each other.

Praise of Each Other

We need to praise each other in our families. Too often, our homes become the outlet only for criticism and frustration.

I once watched in utter dismay as a family across the restaurant from us spent the whole time putting each other down. The father in this apparently blended family kept referring to his wife's "bad kids" and "little stupid kids." As we ate, I felt sick to my stomach. If that's happening in public, what must be happening in private? May God bless our families and our children.

Let your home be a home of praise. Point out each other's good qualities. Have "praise wars" and compliment the socks off each other. It will take intentional focus to accomplish this—but the rewards will be worth it!

Personal Moments

1. How does your family praise God, Jesus, and the Holy Spirit?

2. What do you do to praise each other in your family? If others observed your family, would they say you praise and encourage each other or pick on and put down each other?

3. What will you do to make your home more of a "house of praise"?

QUALITY

Philip B. Crosby, the great quality management guru, taught businesses and manufacturers that quality was defined as conforming to requirements. And he insisted that the way to ensure quality in products and practices was "doing things right the first time." I think this applies to our families. We should aspire to have quality families, and that means conforming to God's requirements for our lives. And the way to ensure that we have quality families is to do things right as best we can, all the time. Doing things right means finding ways to let God work to build our families. Let me explain.

During the summers while I was in college I worked as a brick mason's laborer. I called that slave labor, and the Old Testament backs me up: Those who worked with brick and mortar were slaves for the Egyptians, and my stint as a laborer sure felt that way. Years later, God used that job to show me several principles that apply to building a family.

Psalm 127:1 says, "Unless the Lord builds the house, the builders labor in vain." I've quoted that verse for years because it sounds good, especially for a family speaker. But I didn't fully understand it until I asked the Lord to explain something to me.

The verse refers to both the Lord and others as builders— but if I were going to build a house, I would hire one builder, not two. Then the Lord reminded me of my time as a laborer.

I was not the mason; I did not design the building or lay the brick. But I *did* become a partner in the building process, because the mason could not work without a laborer.

God showed me that he is the mason, the Master Builder, and I am the laborer, or cobuilder.

Let's look at those two jobs—first, that of the laborer.

We must keep all the supplies at his fingertips.
As a laborer, my job was to bring the mason what he needed. If he needed something, he would simply yell out, "Hey, Seaborn, bring me more mortar!"—or whatever.

I believe God looks at our families and says, "Bring that stuff to me. I can only build when you bring the supplies to my hands." This calls for a constant preparedness for whatever situation arises. In practical terms, that means you need to keep God's word in your heart so it can be activated by the Holy Spirit. In that way, you can be prepared every day.

We must have a servant mentality.
A man named Hank was my supervisor at one construction site. He knew I wanted to be a mason, but I'd never had the opportunity. One day he had to leave the site to bid on a future job, so he allowed me to be a mason for the thirty or so minutes he would be away. I remember calling to my buddies—who were now my laborers—"Bring me mud!" or whatever else I needed.

"Dan, I can tell where you started building this wall," Hank said when he returned.

"What do you mean?" I asked.

"Look right here," he said. "It's not as level as it was when I was doing the work. If I leave these bricks that you laid in this wall, when we get to the top of this building we are going to have a problem. The foundation isn't right." And he proceeded to knock all the bricks off. My buddies—my colaborers—laughed at me and taunted me, because I wasn't able to build a wall as well as an experienced mason could.

So many times in my life I have attempted to jerk one of the bricks out of God's hand and say, "Let me put that in my kid's life. I know where that needs to go." And Christ has had to remind me that "unless he builds the house," the masterpiece that would have been my family will be structurally unsound.

This calls for humility, which is tough for me. At times I think God isn't working on my wife or children the way I'd like him to. But the issue isn't them; the issue is *me*. I must be humble and see that Christ wants to work on my life, not theirs.

We must keep the mortar pliable.
Part of my responsibility was to make sure the mortar was the right consistency. If the mortar was too thick, the mason would say, "Seaborn, get some more water and soften the mortar."

As we get older, it's especially important to keep our mortar soft—to stay flexible. Jesus is looking for people who are willing to be molded, challenged, and changed. If we want our children to be willing to be molded, let's set an example by staying pliable for the Lord's use.

Now let's look at the characteristics of the Master Builder: God.

God builds to code.

I asked some people who had completed a huge building what it was like when the inspector came. They said it was a nightmare. He checked wires and depth and accuracy and everything else, over and over again. After hours of analysis, he gave permission to open the building.

If I never allow God to be the builder of my kids' lives, it will take that much longer for God to be able to use them. God knows the code for their lives and the plans he has laid out for them—and his abilities far surpass mine.

> Our children are not ours. We are responsible for their care and training, but one day they will leave our home and establish their own.

God builds brick by brick.

My tendency is to grab a lot of foundational bricks and throw them into my kids' lives. I want them to work on patience, sensitivity, love, and grace at the same time. Jesus says, "Hang on; they can only handle one brick."

He does this with me too. I would love to believe the foundation of my life is finished so I could be done with it all, but the Lord says, "No, I'll build you, Dan, brick by brick."

It's almost as if he places a brick (let's call this one "patience") in my life and begins to tap it. Masons do this—they tap the bricks into place with the end of their trowels. Sometimes Christ taps on the very brick that I wish he would just leave alone.

God makes each structure unique.

Our children are unique, and the Lord has a unique plan for each one.

I once asked two little girls who were identical twins about the things they liked.

"What is your favorite color?"

They both said, "Pink."

"What's your favorite movie?" They named the same Disney movie.

Finally I asked, "What's your favorite food?" One said, "Pizza" and the other, "Pasta."

Even though they looked identical, they had their differences.

He owns the building.

Our children are not ours. We are responsible for their care and training, but one day they will leave our home and establish their own.

I challenge you to analyze your life as a laborer. If you've jumped on the wrong side of the building process, humble yourself and become a servant. Unless Christ builds your home, you will build in vain.

Personal Moments

1. How have you tried to take over the "master-builder" role in your family relationships?
2. What makes you slip from the "laborer-builder" role to the "master-builder" role?
3. What could you do to be a better "laborer-builder?"

4. Does your family spend quality time together? Quantity time? How could you create more of each?

RELAX

This chapter isn't for everyone, because there are plenty of parents out there who are far too relaxed. They don't care about improving their family relationships, and they don't want to exert the effort they know it will take. I've got a word for them—in fact, two words: Wake up!

But on to the rest of you. I know by your willingness to invest time in reading these thoughts that you're actively trying to become a better parent. So why would I tell you to relax? Frankly, because many people who try to be faithful in teaching and training their kids put too much pressure on themselves. There's almost this unspoken, competitive attitude: "I can do more for my kids than you can for yours." And what scares me is that "doing more" translates into "getting more"—trendier cars, bigger houses, faster Internet access. We need to step back and relax a bit.

One of the ways I've helped myself relax is by making sure my children don't have the best of everything. That sounds like pure heresy in the twenty-first century, but my reasoning is this: By doing this, I'm giving them room to improve their lives for themselves. If we give our kids the best of everything, we set them up for failure when they get out into the world on their own.

Recently as I was driving to a speaking engagement, I was thinking about the stages of development I've gone through and what I most looked forward to during each stage. I believe my experiences are typical of those of most people.

> **Many people who try to be faithful in teaching and training their kids put too much pressure on themselves.**

The Stages of "I Can't Wait" Development

Stage 1: "I can't wait until Christmas" (or "my birthday").
Remember when you were a kid? It seemed as if your birthday would never arrive, and the time between Thanksgiving and Christmas seemed like a decade. There was nothing like those days, and we all loved it!

Stage 2: "I can't wait to turn sixteen" (or whatever the driving age is in your state).
It's simply magical, unexplainable. We made it. We're really mature now. We make the best decisions possible, or so we think. People respect us and talk about how big we are and how much we've changed since they last saw us. And we've got money now!

Stage 3: "I can't wait to get my first car."
Some teens bite off stages two and three at the same time. Take a moment and think about the first car you ever owned. You'll never have that first-car feeling again. I remember trying to keep the rain off mine and hating the days when I had

to leave it outside during a storm. I'm forty now and have driven several new cars off the lot, and they still pale in comparison to my first car, a yellow Chevy Nova with eighty thousand miles on it the day I drove it from Deadwyler's Shopping Lot. That felt *so* good.

Stage 4: "I can't wait to get married."

I remember that as our wedding day approached, I was sure something would happen to derail the ceremony. The day kept creeping closer and closer and finally, we made it. And there's no day that passes quicker than this one. All the months and months of planning pass in an instant. Then there's that honeymoon thing—don't get me started on that!

Stage 5: "I can't wait to have our first child."

That day can't come quickly enough, especially for a dear woman who has moved into the third trimester. After all the preparations—getting the nursery ready, reading up on parenting skills, preparing your heart—there you are in the delivery room. It's an incredible feeling … and then before you know it, you've got four more kids!

Stage 6: "I can't wait for our first grandchild to come along."

I can speak from experience here, because this is the stage I'm in right now. Sure, there are a lot of other cool things that can happen in your life, but based on what I've heard from first-time grandparents, this is right up there with the coolest. I can't wait.

Stage 7: "I can't wait to see heaven."

This is simply a final stage in the maturing process. My mother is there. She loves life and enjoys being with us, but she has experienced all this world has to offer and is prepared for the next. I used to hear my grandparents say they couldn't wait for heaven, but at the time I didn't understand how they could feel that way. As I grow older, that sentiment is coming into focus for me. And I'm glad. It's normal.

So here's the purpose of this whole "stage of development" process: It helps us understand how we mature into more eternal thinking and less temporal thinking. If that isn't happening, we need to analyze our priorities. As we do that, we can allow ourselves to relax and enjoy parenting, and allow our children to enjoy their own stages of development.

As I was thinking through my personal stages of development, I realized how much I want my children to enjoy each one. Parents often rush their children through these stages and almost try to force them to respond the way they want them to during each stage. But the wise, relaxed parent will step back and give his or her children freedom to develop on their own. What they need is a hands-off, heart-on involvement, one that incorporates prayer, encouragement, grace, love, and daily care.

I hope this has helped you relive some great memories and relax a bit. My wife and I are learning to relax more with each of our children. That's difficult to accomplish in a "do more" society, but parents who have learned to relax will experience the joys of family life more fully.

Personal Moments

1. What stages are you in as a family? Write the name of each family member and his or her stage of development.
2. What other stages would you include that have been significant in your life?
3. How successful are you in allowing others to experience these stages without interfering?
4. What kinds of things stress you out? Consider things you could do to relax more.

SELFLESSNESS

There are many other "S" words I could have chosen—like *servanthood, sacrifice, surrender, solitude* (my personal favorite)— but nothing hits the bull's-eye quite like *selflessness.* This is a foundational word for family success. A selfish family is a destructive family; a selfless family is a devoted family. A selfish family is an unsatisfied family; a selfless family is a contented family.

The reason selflessness is strategic is because selfishness is the exact opposite of God. Any self-promotion, self-focus, or self-desire is therefore a force working against family harmony and obedience to God. Selfishness must not be tolerated within the family structure. Parents must model selflessness on a consistent basis and emphasize the concept with their children.

I recently traveled to a speaking engagement with a friend who told me this story. It was dinnertime at his home, and one of his three children—I'll call him Jeff—had been playing a computer game. As they ate, Jeff's brother—"Mike," for our purposes—asked if he could play the game after dinner. "Sure, no problem," Jeff said. But after the meal, Jeff ran right back to the computer, prompting Mike to cry and throw a tantrum.

My friend lost his cool and exploded onto the scene. He proceeded to rant and rave for a long time, causing an uproar in the whole family.

> ## Any self-promotion, self-focus, or self-desire is therefore a force working against family harmony and obedience to God.

This scene sounds all too familiar to me—and probably to you as well. I've witnessed scenarios like this, and I've even initiated them. And the reason they occur is selfishness. While the initial act of selfishness does not justify everyone else's negative behavior, that one act did instigate the resulting chaos.

After a cool-down period, Jeff said, "Dad, I'm sorry. I knew I should have let him play, but I couldn't stop myself."

Sound familiar again? It's natural to be selfish, to be bent toward what we want and to ignore the needs and wants of others.

One method we've used to counter this problem in our family is to give the offender—and the rest of us—a "theme" word to live by.

This is how our method works. Every so often we, as a family, need to be challenged in order to get to the next level, individually and corporately. So, through prayer and discussion, Jane and I seek the Lord's guidance in developing theme words for each family member to adopt and live by for a set period of time. Here are some of the words and phrases that we recently assigned to family members: calm, joyful selflessness, strong leader, happy obedience, discipline.

After Jane and I decided on the words, we had a little family pow-wow and shared these concepts and thoughts with the children, explaining them at each child's level of understanding. For the younger children, we wrote the word on a cardboard or decorative sheet and put it on their bed. At night we would pray for that particular characteristic to grow in their lives.

This activity has had a big impact on our children's behavior and on us. Specifically, the one child who had been assigned the "joyful selflessness" theme showed remarkable progress in that area in the first week of the process.

I believe the personal challenge, along with the opportunity to put their hands on an issue, helped our children to change their behavior. Of course, the work of the Holy Spirit is the unseen force that brings about all internal change. But the children cooperated.

The bottom line is that we cannot allow selfishness to infect our homes. Selfishness will destroy all our positive efforts; it must be replaced by selflessness.

Here is a catch phrase to remember: In our homes, *fish less!* In other words, change the sel*fish* to self*less*. It's just a four-letter change, but it requires a serious attitude adjustment.

Personal Moments

1. Would the atmosphere in your family be defined as selfless or selfish?
2. What are some specific things that create selfishness in your family? Selflessness?
3. How can you move toward greater selflessness within your family?

    a. Define specific things each family member could do to grow in selflessness.

    b. Celebrate some things you've done that were selfless.

4. Ask the Holy Spirit to heighten your awareness in this area of your life. Pray for a servant's heart and attitude.

T

TRUST

Trust is one of the most important gifts we can give to our spouse and to our children. When I meet with couples after one partner has been unfaithful, I am amazed at the amount of distrust that has built up. It takes years for the unfaithful spouse to earn his or her partner's trust again. I remember seeing "Karen" just after she had been unfaithful to her husband. She wanted her husband's trust in her restored right *now*, and he wanted to go out and even the score.

I've also counseled men who had been unfaithful and expected their wives to trust them completely within a few weeks. That's simply not possible. And when we are unfaithful or in some other way lose our spouse's trust, we cause our children to become anxious. They wonder if *they* can trust us anymore. If we've been unfaithful to each other, what's to stop us from being unfaithful to them?

A foundation of trust in God is essential to trusting each other.

There's a passage in the Bible that David wrote to celebrate his victory over Goliath. In it, he looks beyond his own victory to the victory God would give him in the end over his enemies. Psalm 9:7-10 reads,

> The Lord reigns forever; he has established his throne for judgment. He will judge the world in righteousness;

he will govern the peoples with justice. The Lord is a refuge for the oppressed, a stronghold in times of trouble. Those who know your name will trust in you, for you, Lord, have never forsaken those who seek you.

This passage doesn't say that the Lord reigns for a certain period of time or until we decide not to let him reign anymore. You can trust in the fact that the Lord will reign forever. In that same vein, your kids, your spouse, and your extended family all need to know they can trust you. We will never attain the level of trust God provides, yet we must seek to be faithful. If trust is lost, all is lost.

There are four things this passage teaches us about our relationships with God and with our family.

1. Trust involves believing that the Lord reigns forever.

As David approached Goliath with a sling, I imagine the Israelites didn't feel as if the Lord was reigning. A feeble little boy up against the monster Goliath? Sometimes I feel like a little boy with a sling, trying to destroy monstrous issues in my family. In those moments I have to remind myself that the Lord reigns forever. In the midst of difficult times, we may not *feel* that the Lord is reigning. But Psalm 9:7 does not say that you have to *feel* like the Lord is reigning. Instead, it simply says "the Lord reigns forever." He does. That's the verdict. That's the end of it.

Put on the wall of your family life a statement that reads, "The Lord is in control of our family. We can trust him." That means Dad and Mom are going to be faithful to each other and stick together. It means Dad and Mom are going to love their children unconditionally. The trust that results is powerful enough to bind your family together.

> **You can trust in the fact that the Lord will reign forever. In that same vein, your kids, your spouse, and your extended family all need to know they can trust you.**

2. Trust involves knowing that the Lord judges in righteousness and governs with justice.

Psalm 9:8 says: "He will judge the world in righteousness; He will govern the peoples with justice." As I read the newspaper and see the injustice that permeates our society, I rejoice in knowing that there *is* a standard that we are all going to be held to. There will come a day when all wrongs will be made right and all injustice will be terminated. We need to remember that as we teach our children. Why do we have a moral code in our home? Because we believe there is a moral responsibility and there is a day coming when we will have to answer for the way we have lived.

What a great lesson to teach our children. Trust that God will someday confirm this teaching and that the way we live today will determine what will happen to us on that day.

3. Trust involves understanding that the Lord is a refuge and a stronghold.

God sometimes may seem to put our families in a vise grip. He tightens down on us; we don't like the pressure, we don't like the strain, and we certainly don't like the pain. But we can trust in the fact that he will hold us. I haven't always liked the pressure that I feel him putting on me, but he is holding me secure in my relationship with him. You can trust him, even if it sometimes feels like a vise grip. He is a stronghold. He is a refuge.

Maybe your family is facing a trial beyond your control. According to his word, he is there for you, being that refuge and stronghold today.

4. Trust involves knowing his name and abiding in him.

His name has withstood the test of time, the test of persecution, the test of prosperity, the test of disbelief. His name has simply withstood.

Our family was once in a particularly difficult time when many little things hit us at once. My wife and I found ourselves disagreeing; the kids were more edgy than normal. My oldest son even asked, "Dad, what's going on?"

I said, "Son, we need to have a family pow-wow, go to the Lord, and remember that it's in his name that we can find the strength we need." That evening we gathered around the table and talked about how Satan wanted to destroy our family, while Christ wanted to give us an abiding strength. We asked the Lord to remind us that his name was what held us together.

Trust begins with God and then moves into our home.

Personal Moments

1. What things have happened in your home that have built up trust? Eroded trust?

2. How have you let the Lord influence your family's level of trust?

3. What could each of you do to build more trust within your family? (Possibilities include such things as being faithful and honest in your relationships, never deceiving one another, never putting one another down.)

UNDERSTANDING

This word can be a life-changer for families. Look no further than Proverbs 24:1-4 for proof: "By wisdom a house is built, and through understanding it is established; through knowledge its rooms are filled with rare and beautiful treasures."

Understanding establishes a home, making it strong and secure. Families that are strong and secure seem to be the exception rather than the rule today. That's because God alone provides the strength and security we need in our family relationships and so few families seem willing to turn to him.

Psalm 111:10 gives us insight into the concept of biblical understanding by stating that "all who follow his precepts have good understanding." But what are his precepts? Precepts are the laws, rules, and guidelines God gives us in his word that provide the basic principles for living.

Among the precepts every family needs to obey are the Ten Commandments. Some people consider these Old Testament precepts to be outdated and irrelevant to the family of the new millennium. I'd like to put a positive spin on these ancient laws by presenting a fresh new way of looking at the Ten Commandments.

> **God's word is where true insight begins and where we develop strength and security in our family relationships.**

In fact, we'll call this

Ten Wonderful Guiding Commands for Families

I. God is number one in our home.
We will do everything we can to keep God first. When other stuff starts creeping in, we will discuss ways we can keep God in the forefront of our lives.

II. We will keep "stuff" in proper perspective.
God has given us everything we need. Our family will share our earthly possessions with others and never value things over people.

III. We will talk about God in positive ways.
Our goal is to speak of God's greatness. There will be difficult times, and we will call on him for guidance. There will be times of blessing, and we will give him praise. We must work diligently to keep our home a place where God is glorified in our language.

IV. We will set aside one day every week for worship and rest.
God designed us to work hard but also recognized our need for rest. We will worship God, and then our family will decide which activities are suitable for this "holy" day.

V. We will honor and respect our parents.
Believing that God has given our parents wisdom and under-standing, we will love and care for them as long as they live. We also recognize that God teaches us to build our own home

separate from our parents, something we will do to set an example for our children and our children's children.

VI. We will be pro-life.

We believe that whether it's unborn babies, the elderly, the disabled, or the incredibly healthy, all are created by God and deserve the right to live.

VII. Mom and Dad will be faithful to each other.

One of the most beautiful gifts couples can give to each other and to their children is fidelity in marriage. We will pray for the Lord's protection over our marriage and home, and flee from temptations when they arise. We will pray together to build additional stability in all our relationships.

VIII. We will use only what is ours or what is lent to us.

God has given us all we need, and he promises he will care for us as he does the birds of the air. When others help us, we will consider their actions to be a blessing from God.

IX. We will speak words of truth about others.

Our neighbors, our relatives, our friends, and our enemies deserve our best. We will always speak truthfully about them.

X. We will live satisfied.

If our house isn't the biggest, if our car isn't the nicest, if our cupboards aren't the fullest—no problem, we are satisfied. This is an attitude we will choose to have every day.

Now consider what would happen if families, one by one, adopted this fresh paraphrase of the Ten Commandments. Homes would be restored, neighborhoods would come alive with love, and towns and cities would be radically changed. Half the newspaper headlines would be deleted if we began to follow these guidelines. If our family obeyed these principles, some unwanted headlines would be deleted from our family life as well. These precepts fit every generation and every home.

God's word is the first place we should go to find understanding. That is where true insight begins and where we develop strength and security in our family relationships. God provides a biblical understanding and helps us attain a human understanding. Through seeking him for this understanding, obeying his precepts, and allowing individuality in others, we deepen our relationships with each other.

Personal Moments

1. What is the basis for understanding that you use in your home? Is it one parent's belief system, what you learned from your own parents—or does it change each day? Do you seek God daily for his understanding?

2. What are some of the precepts of God that you apply naturally in your family life? Are your children adopting these principles and practicing them in their personal life?

3. How understanding are you of the needs of your children? Of the needs of your spouse? When others don't agree with your opinions? When difficult problems arise?

VENTILATION

If you've ever painted the inside of your home, you know the importance of ventilation. Without those openings for fresh air to enter to allow the room to "breathe," the rooms can be stifling. Ventilation, in the context of this chapter, means giving yourself room to breathe in your family relationships. Here are several steps to good ventilation, a way to help you breathe as a parent.

Stop trying to be perfect.
When I felt called to a family-oriented ministry, I thought I was too young. The Lord showed me he would help others through my mistakes. I didn't exactly celebrate that, but I've since realized how valuable it is to identify with another person's problems.

Psalm 15:2 says: "He whose walk is blameless and who does what is righteous will dwell in the Lord's sanctuary." It doesn't say we need to be perfect, only blameless—guilt-free. If anyone does a background check on me, they'll find I've already confessed my failures and I've had plenty to acknowledge.

Most parents live with feelings of guilt over things they wish they had done differently. We can't control the past, but we can help control our future by the decisions we make today. We begin by saying, "I don't have to be perfect, just blameless."

Make time for recreation.

Parents who don't take breaks don't give their kids a break. They are simply too stressed. You need time to develop as a parent and a spouse, and one way to do that is to get away. If possible, take some extended time away from your children. It gives you rest and helps you refocus.

An at-home mom who doesn't get out with her friends or take time for herself is no doubt stressed-out and lonely. A dad who works all day, does the dad thing at night, and never takes a break for himself is probably on the brink. When we get away and have some space for ventilation, we become better parents.

Understand your own rules.

If you are going to have rules, enforce them. If you skirt around the rules, your children will learn to push your buttons. When they're older, they won't be able to establish boundaries for themselves.

Establishing rules requires the discipline to implement them and protects you from countless battles down the road. It also takes the burden off your shoulders and places it on your children, who are now responsible for following the rules. But if you play out every situation as if it was a court case, you're asking for trouble.

> Parents who don't take breaks don't give their kids a break. They are simply too stressed.

Let kids be kids.

They will make messes, and they will break things. I tend to treat our children like adults. The Lord once showed me that I would be less stressed if I followed these guidelines:

Have realistic expectations. Consider your children's ages, and don't expect everything to be in order each day when you come home.

Plan on something breaking once a week. We don't try to meet this quota, but we do prepare for accidents. That reduces some of the stress.

When something does break, don't go crazy. Like many parents, I had trained my kids to feel afraid if they broke something. Thankfully, I've changed that.

Watch for unhealthy ruts.

Here are a few:

- yelling
- couch loafing
- noncommunication
- sarcasm
- avoiding home as much as possible

In 1 Thessalonians 3:7, Paul writes that Timothy "told us you always have pleasant memories of us." I want our children to have pleasant memories of our home, to think of it as a place where they were allowed to be themselves.

Seek help.

One of the best things you can do as a parent is admit you don't know it all and tell your children that. They already know when you don't know something; they just need to hear you admit it.

When you don't handle a situation well, ventilate what you are thinking. Then give your family an opportunity to breathe back on you some words of wisdom that will help you. Rely on other adults who believe in you and can help you talk through the myriad issues of parenting. Enlist a grandparent, teacher, friend, or godparent to talk with your kids if necessary.

Share child-care responsibilities.

Knowing other adults who are willing to spend time with your children and invest in them is critical. Recently, another couple took care of our children while my wife and I went away for four days. We're just as willing to take their children into our house. Tradeoffs like that help each couple take a break and allow the children to experience different family styles.

Talk with your spouse about improving your family.

Jane and I go away twice a year to reexamine and talk about our marriage relationship and parenting skills. I encourage you to take advantage of a getaway like this. So many couples tell me that they are afraid to talk about areas where they struggle because they don't want to get into an argument. But if you agree to have an open and loving conversation, the resulting ventilation can make an incredible difference.

Recognize recurring patterns.

For our family, one week into the school year marks a time when we all get edgy with each other. Suddenly we are back on a schedule we're not used to. Now, in preparation for that, about two weeks before school begins I remind our kids how much our lives are going to change in the next month. This allows us to ventilate and prepares the kids for the start of school.

Many families go on vacation and spend the first day arguing and fighting. That's another recurring pattern, so it would be wise to take time before a vacation to share your expectations.

Recognizing those cycles in your family will help you prepare for them.

Be a kid every now and then.

Many parents don't laugh at themselves or have fun with their kids. One of the memories I want my children to have is hearing lots of laughter in our home. Sometimes you just need to be a kid again. You are going to make mistakes; give yourself some breathing room. Family mishaps can lead to arguments, or they can lead to ventilation and good-natured laughter. The second path will help keep your family strong.

These are simple ideas that will give you a little breathing room within your family.

Personal Moments

1. Take time to think and talk about these ideas. Are you implementing any of them already? Do you have good "ventilation" in your family, or are you "stifled"?

2. What is the obvious thing you could begin to do today to give each other a little breathing room?

3. Let each family member express (ventilate) what would be helpful to him or her in terms of a little breathing room.

WISDOM

I'm not sure where Jane picked up this quote, but every now and then—usually when I'm working really hard at improving my skills as a father and husband—she will say to me, "Dan, don't forget, 'A smart man learns from his mistakes; a wise man learns from someone else's mistakes.'" That's my motto! I've made lots of mistakes and will make many more, but I'm determined to learn from the mistakes of others so I won't have to make all of them myself.

Wisdom—the ability to make sound judgments and decisions based on godly principles—comes from God himself. James 1:5 says, "If any of you lacks wisdom, he should ask God, who gives generously to all without finding fault, and it will be given to him."

I am one who prays for wisdom from God. I pray for wisdom to know and understand my wife. I pray for wisdom to know and understand my children. The idea of praying for wisdom is found in the Bible; you can be assured that you will receive wisdom when you ask God for it.

> There are many smart people who make foolish, foolish mistakes.

There's a big difference between being wise and being smart. There are many smart people who make foolish, foolish mistakes. I was thinking about this as I was driving one day and noticed the signs people place in their yards. Some of them seem to correspond to the way different families live their lives. Here's what I mean:

For Sale by Owner
Some people put their families up for sale. They decide they want another family, or they're just tired of hanging out with the one they have; it's time for something new. Others have sold out their families because of their addiction to alcohol, drugs, gambling, or sex. But you cannot sell what you do not own, and you cannot own other people.

For Lease or Rent
Shortly after the Columbine High School shootings, radio commentator Paul Harvey listed the many factors that have contributed to the disintegration of the home: half of our children are raised in broken homes; children spend an average of thirty seconds in meaningful conversation with their parents each day; they watch, on average, seven hours of sex- and violence-filled television each day and play video games that involve killing as many opponents as possible in the most sadistic way possible; they are so spoiled that they equate love with receiving material things. He continued on with point after point after point that drove home the impact of the failure of parents and society to value the lives of children.

What he said comes down to this: We have leased out our

children and rented out our families. We have allowed decay to cause a major disintegration in our families. As a society, we think we are so smart, but we've failed to heed the warning signs that lead to tragedy.

Keep Out!

Like you, I've met many people who say, "I don't want God to be a part of my life." On a recent TV show, a very hostile man said, "Oh, you are saying that I must accept *your* Christ." I wanted to scream at him, "No, he's not *my* Christ, he's *our* Christ!" People choose to reject him—and let me tell you, this is not a wise thing to do!

The Bible teaches us in Psalm 111:10 that "the fear of the Lord is the beginning of wisdom." The word fear in this context means great awe and respect. Wisdom begins to take root in our lives when we understand that we are accountable to God—to respect him, to reverence him, to acknowledge him with our lives.

Open House

Some people open their homes up to many kinds of spiritual forces, all in the name of tolerance. But the very people who want Christians to be tolerant of other belief systems are often those who are the least tolerant of the Christian belief system! Remember, too, that if we open our minds up to every idea that is out there, our brains could fall out.

Wisdom does not come from being open to every idea that's offered. Wisdom comes from having a balance in our life and understanding where true wisdom comes from.

Every family should memorize and use Proverbs 24:3 as their foundation. That verse says, "By wisdom a house is built." That's pretty simple, but it makes a profound statement about the foundation a house should be built upon.

I once was invited to speak to a group of corporate leaders on balancing home life with work. A well-known doctor gave his presentation right before mine. He was terrific; he used lots of big words and really seemed to know his stuff. The audience gave him a standing ovation, then sat down to listen to the next speaker—me.

That doctor was a tough act to follow, but everyone seemed to be very attentive to my presentation. I felt they had begun to connect with everything I had to say. Yet no more than five minutes into my speech, this well-educated, highly regarded doctor, so valued for his intelligence and his education, stood up, waved his arm toward me, and said, "What a waste of my time!" As he walked out of the room, the people watched him and then looked back at me as if to ask, "What are you going to do about that?"

Well, I got so fired up that you would have thought I'd been hit with a jolt of electricity. I began to go after my topic with two hands, waving them around and telling those people that they *must* balance their home life; they *must* make sure their education isn't more important than their family; they *must* make sure their work doesn't run their family into the muck. When I finished, thanks to the Lord, I also received an overwhelming ovation.

That doctor may have been smart, but he wasn't very wise. I wondered if his children would have encouraged him to pay attention to what I said instead of scoffing at me, because they missed having Dad around.

My grandfather never got farther than elementary school, but he was one of the wisest men I ever knew! Not because he used big words or could spell onomatopoeia or knew what a hypotenuse was, but because he knew how to love and care for his family even as he ran a fairly large farm.

I'm grateful for men like him who have shown me, by their example, the difference between being smart and being wise. They're the ones who have the right to place the best sign of all, right in the middle of their front yard: Model Home.

That should be our goal, to build a model home, a model family, for all the world to see. That's a goal that's founded on wisdom.

Personal Moments

1. What does "guiding a home with wisdom" mean to you?
2. What could you do to be a wiser parent?
3. Which of these phrases best describes your home as illustrated in this chapter?
   - For Sale by Owner
   - For Lease or Rent
   - Keep Out!
   - Open House
   - Model Home

XEROGAPOGYS!

Don't even bother looking that word up in the dictionary. It doesn't exist. I made it up to emphasize the importance of thinking outside the confines of our known vocabulary. Because that's what our families need to realize: There is more to each family than meets the eye, more than anything that can be confined to what is supposedly known about each family. Your family has some unique characteristics and traits that are yours alone, and you can use that to your advantage.

I am sometimes guilty of comparing our family to others, wondering, "My goodness, why can't we accomplish as much as *that* family does?" and "Why don't we have as much stuff as *this* family has?" and "Wouldn't it be nice to travel as many places as *they* do?" If you get into that comparison game, pretty soon you will become dissatisfied with what you have and how you live. Naturally, that leads to an atmosphere of gloom and doom within your entire family.

Start to analyze the unique things about your family and use those things to build a stronger family unit. If you're not sure just what it is that makes your family the unique unit it is, you can discover those traits by asking several questions.

What is something your family is good at?

Think about the different things you do as a family. Celebrate what you are good at. When we compare ourselves to others, we are constantly trying to live up to someone else's standard. Odds are pretty good there is another family out there trying to be like yours, so make sure your standard is high.

Maybe your greatest gift is something that is unseen. That's fine! Maybe your greatest gift is servanthood. That's wonderful! You may not get famous or rich with that, but you can't beat servanthood as a means of showing your children what's important in life.

Psychologists show people how to intentionally delete their negative thought patterns by taping over them with positive thoughts. Most families focus far too much on their negative traits rather than on the positive gifts God has blessed them with. Spend time as a family discussing the things that you do well, and come up with ways you can do those things even better.

What is a unique thing your family does, or the unique story you have to tell?

We recently celebrated a holiday with some friends. There were about a dozen families represented. A few weeks before the party, the host had asked each family to send in six statements that expressed something unusual about their current situation or their family history. Some of the things sent in were, "My grandfather was a full-blooded Cherokee Indian" and "I come from a long line of prostitutes." The host would read a statement, and the rest of us would try to guess which person or family it described. We had a blast, and our family came away with a nickname, which I refuse to share.

I'll bet your children don't know some of the bizarre or funny things from your family's history. What a great time you could have sharing with your children the stories your parents told you! Try it; you might be amazed at how it helps your children understand who you are and where you came from.

Ask others what they think is really cool about your family. This may seem a little awkward and weird at first, but I can guarantee that other people say things about your family that you never realized. Isn't it funny that we don't hear those types of things ourselves? Usually it's through the grapevine that we find out what others think of us, whether it's good or bad. So be aggressive. Be proactive. Let others help you discover what some of your best qualities are and try to influence other people in those areas. I believe God wants each family to accomplish something great; sometimes, it's easier for others to identify what that is.

It's fun to think about the different families we've known as neighbors and the influence they've had on our lives, without even trying to be any kind of influence at all. In South Carolina, the Babcocks influenced us in the area of household and property maintenance, sharing valuable information with us about how to take care of our lawn and keep our house in good repair. In Michigan, the Velthouse family taught us, by their example, how to spend time together as a family and make the best use of dinnertime as a special teaching and learning time together.

I also remember another family, who will remain nameless, that gave us an example of what it means to focus too much on the material things you own rather than on the living, breathing people in your house. We don't want to follow that example. Without realizing it, they helped us understand how important it is to steer clear of focusing on stuff.

I imagine that if you take a moment you could describe, in two or three words, the families that live around you and the families you've lived near in the past. Trust me, those families have a couple of words they can use to describe yours as well. What would those words be? What do you think your family looks like to other people?

Your family is special and has talents and abilities that no other family has. You live in a specific neighborhood, and you have the power to influence that neighborhood like no one else does. You can make a mark on this world in a way that no other family can. So take advantage of it! Quit thinking you have to be like everybody else! Think outside the twenty-six letters of the alphabet, outside the vocabulary that's been provided for you. Make your own letter and word, uniquely marking this earth with your family's talents.

> **You can make a mark on this world in a way that no other family can.**

Personal Moments

1. What are some of the unique things about your family? Characteristics? Names? Hobbies? Stories?
2. Talk about these traits as a family. Celebrate your uniqueness! Give your family a unique name.
3. Make sure you laugh at yourself!

YES

Have you ever noticed how often you say "no"? I say it way too much!

"Dad, can I have a snack?" "No."

"Dad, can I go to Brian's house tonight?" "No."

"Dad, do you want to go outside and play?" "No. I'm busy."

I'm convinced our children hear "no" a lot more than they hear "yes." And not just my children, but my wife too.

It's about time we started saying "yes" more.

"Yes, I've got time for you."

"Yes, we can go out tonight just for the fun of it."

"Yes, I'll take tomorrow off from work."

"Yes, we can go get an ice cream cone."

Believe me, I know how hard it is to say "yes" sometimes. Many of us are overworked, overcommitted, and overstressed. Often, it's impossible to say "yes," because we can't take off work tomorrow and we don't have any money for ice cream cones and if we don't do the laundry tonight no one will have clothes to wear to work or school tomorrow.

Single parents in particular know how hard it can be to say "yes" and how painful it is to always have to say "no." I understand your situation, as well as I possibly can without living it. Please don't take this as a setup for another guilt trip. I'm talking mainly to parents who *can* say "yes" but don't, sometimes

---

simply out of habit. We get so accustomed to believing we don't have enough time for anything that we forget that an indispensable part of a healthy childhood is time spent with parents.

Fatigue is another reason—and in many ways a legitimate one—we say "no" so often to our kids. We're bone-tired after working all day, whether in a traditional job or at home, and the last thing we feel like doing is taking the kids out or playing horsey with them or reading the same book to them for what has to be the millionth time. We begin to nod off at the mere thought of all that.

Yet as so many parents have learned, there will come a day, far too soon, when your kids may not want to be seen with you and they'll be too old for horsey and they'll be reading on their own. No, you don't get to sleep then either, because you'll have a long roster of other activities involving your kids, but you'll think back fondly to the days when the activities were simpler—and you'll wish you had cherished the time when your children were young.

Regret is a terrible thing to live with. We can't do anything to change the circumstances that caused us to make regrettable choices in the past, but we can start to make decisions right now that we won't regret in the future. Have you ever heard a parent regret having spent so much time with their kids when they were young? Probably not. But it's likely you've heard the opposite—parents who wish they could relive those years, who have realized far too late just how meaningless all those things were that prevented them from saying "yes" to their children more often.

We need to consciously cultivate a yes spirit. We can start by applying a bit of math to our children's requests: For every time we say "no," we need to say "yes" two times or three times or whatever number of times it takes to change our negative tone to a positive one and to instill a "yes" habit into our responses.

But it needs to go deeper than that. Yes has to seep way down into our spirit so we no longer have to do the math, so that saying "yes" is as natural as breathing. Does that mean we'll be saying "yes" all the time, spoiling our kids, running ourselves ragged, and booking a room at the poorhouse? No. It means that we will instinctively know when to say "yes."

To cultivate that yes spirit, we also have to remember what's important. Here are two more ways you can jump-start your yes approach to your children's requests; both will help you remember what's important.

> **For every time we say "no," we need to say "yes" two times or three times or whatever number of times it takes to change our negative tone.**

Slow Down and Listen

The phone is ringing. The fax machine is spitting out sheets of paper. The microwave is beeping its announcement to hurry up and open the door. Every bell and whistle in the world seems to be vying for our attention. Meanwhile, there's a little person quietly tugging at our sleeve. Will we turn our attention to the bells and whistles—or to the little person we brought into this noisy world?

Some of the best experiences we'll ever have with our children occur when we least expect it. Too often we try to make the moment happen—we think a trip to Disney World will do the trick. But it won't. We have our own magic kingdom at home, the delightful and captivating world of our kids. When we slow down and listen to them, those precious and irreplaceable moments come to us naturally. "Yes," we need to say, "I've got time to play a game with you." And then we need to become fully engaged with their world, forgetting ours for the time being.

Play the "What If?" Game

Speaking of games, here's a good one for parents: the "What If?" game. Ask yourself questions like these: What if I knew today would be my last day with my family? What attitude would I have? Would I have said "yes" to things I said "no" to? Obviously, you can't say "yes" and let everything else go to pieces. But I'll bet you could say "yes" more than you do.

Or play "What's the worst that could happen?" Those questions go like this: What's the worst that could happen if I *did* take off work tomorrow to be with my family? If I *did* round everybody up for a ride to the ice cream stand? If I *did* start reading a book to them the millionth time through? Would it really be all that bad?

Let's commit ourselves to saying "yes" more often. It's a great word—only three letters, and it takes very little breath! Let's let our homes be filled with the positive joy that saying "yes" brings.

Personal Moments

1. What do you hear yourself saying to your family most often—yes or no?

2. Where and when could you say "yes" more? How would it change your lifestyle or habits? Are you willing to make those changes?

3. What would be the short- and long-term benefits to your family or marriage if you said "yes" more often?

Z

ZANY

How appropriate, as we wrap up our journey together, to let the last leg of our trip focus on having some great times by bringing a little zaniness to our family life.

Every family could use a dose of craziness, especially if someone in the family is like me. I'm the kind of guy who believes life is serious—you have to stay focused, and you need to know what type of mark you are making for your family and for the Lord. Yet you'd better be able to cut loose and have a lot of fun along the way; otherwise, as they say, you just become obnoxious. You don't want that to happen, so if you haven't injected your family life with a bit of nuttiness, now's a good time to start.

Maybe you've been reading along since the letter A, and you've been thinking, "This all sounds great, and I'd love to get started, but I just don't know what to do." Well, here you have it: a list of things you can do with your family that are fun and memorable and downright silly. Pick one or two of them, and give it a shot!

> **If you haven't injected your family life with a bit of nuttiness, now's a good time to start.**

How to Be a Little Zany

— The next time you go to a fast-food drive-through, place a sign on the speaker that reads, "Please yell! We can hardly hear you!" Then go inside and listen to the customers yell through the speaker system as they place their orders. You'll have a hoot—just make sure it's a place where the order-takers don't wear headsets!

— Buy some of those "Billy Bob" buckteeth that are advertised on television, and go into a restaurant with your family sporting your new set of chops. I did this recently, and as the waitress approached our table, I said, "I need to eat something that won't make my teeth fall out." Then I looked up and smiled. My kids went nuts, and the waitress started laughing. We had a great time at that table, even though Jane had taken refuge underneath it. I finally convinced her to come up and sit with us. That evening, as we were leaving the restaurant, Anna, who was six at the time, said, "Dad, you are a lot of fun!" I want to continue to be the kind of dad who brings that type of fun to his family life.

— Build a Frisbee course in your yard and your neighbors' yards. We got permission from several neighbors to put signs on trees and fence posts so we could make a golf course-type of playing field for Frisbee players. It's been great! We've seen other families come over and enjoy the course as well. Sometimes it gets a little crazy when several families start competing, but it's a blast!

— Put a "Finally Married!" sign on the back of your car and load up all the kids. Drive right through downtown, honking your horn and laughing like crazy. If you can convince them to, get the kids to wave out the window to show that they're celebrating the fact that their mom and dad finally got married. You may have to go someplace where no one knows you, but have fun with it anyway!

— Tell your kids that you just absolutely, positively *have* to rent another video game. Insist that they go with you to the rental store. Make a big deal out of picking one out, and be sure that you are the first one that gets to play it when you get home.

— Bring home birthday gifts for everybody. (Make sure it's no one's birthday!) Just have a great time opening the gifts, most of which you picked up at the local dollar store, of course.

— Tell your kids that you are going to wake them up and have a pillow fight at 2 A.M. or whatever time works best for your family. Or just do something else unexpected in the middle of the night. When you're all good and exhausted from the festivities, roll out the sleeping bags or quilts and crash together on the floor.

— See who can tell the best joke. During dinner one night, take time to let everybody share something funny. Decide whose joke or story is the best; whoever wins doesn't have to help with the dishes.

— Test-drive a Mercedes or Maserati. Take your whole family down to the dealership and tell the salesperson you need to check out one of those fancy cars. They may insist on riding along with you, but it would still be worth the laugh as you and your family have a great time taking a luxury car for a test drive. (It helps if you know the dealer, of course, since some salespeople may not appreciate the joke!)

— Rent a Santa suit and take gifts to needy kids at Christmastime. You will have a great time, and your children will love going along with you as you deliver gifts to needy children.

I have a friend named Merv who loves to play practical jokes on his family on April Fool's Day. For one of his recent pranks, he conspired with the staff at a local restaurant to stage a huge argument with a waitress when he brought his wife in for dinner—knowing that one of his wife's pet peeves is seeing customers give waitresses a hard time. During their meal, he began to berate the waitress and question everything she did, to the point where the waitress appeared to be in tears. His wife was absolutely furious! To finish off the evening, he got the waitress to confess her part in the prank. If you ask Merv's wife to tell about the funniest thing that's happened to her in the past few years, she'll describe that incident.

Only you know whether that kind of practical joke would go over well in your family. But even if you can't see yourself doing something like Merv did, you can find ways to make your family laugh out loud and have a great time. I know way too many families and way too many individuals who never seem to laugh. I feel sorry for people like that, because they never give themselves the chance to have the kinds of experiences that end up in uncontrollable laughter. Those times are simply unforgettable.

Sit down as a family and talk about some fun activities that you haven't tried before. Even better, come up with some ideas for nutty things you can spring on your family spontaneously.

Believe me, this could completely change the atmosphere of your home. Being zany is a requirement if you want to be a family that keeps their wits about them when everybody else seems to be losing theirs!

Final Moments

1. How has this book helped you? Your family?
2. How will you practice living out some of the principles you've learned?
3. If you are involved in mentoring, how can you take it up another step in your family?

AFTERWORD

I hope this book has given you new energy and vision for your family. Now you may be asking, Where do I go from here? Here are some suggestions.

First, remember we're all a work in progress. Don't get bogged down in negative analysis of the faults in your family. This book should never be taken as a burdensome list of things to do.

You may wish to read this book again and consider what changes would benefit your family the most. Take time with each chapter and even work with your spouse or another individual to develop new habits that will improve your family life.

Second, keep looking to Christ as a source of strength and guidance for yourself and your family. Draw from his wisdom daily, and rest in his strength to carry out his desires through you.

Third, stay on the journey, despite any setbacks you may have. The fact that you've read this book is affirmation that you're headed in the right direction.

And by all means, enjoy your family. Laugh together. Have fun growing up together, and know that God is with you every step of the way.

Winning At Home

Our Vision and Mission:

Winning At Home, Inc. is a non-profit organization with a vision to reach around the world with practical biblical insight for today's families, challenging them to a closer relationship with Jesus Christ and each other. Our vision here at Winning At Home is to encourage people at all ages and stages of family development to lead Christ-centered homes. We seek to do this through radio programming, conference speaking, books and other multi-media resources all designed to offer hope and renewal to individual lives.

Radio programs:

Family Stuff—a thirteen-minute Christian radio program that introduces a fresh approach to family issues. Dan Seaborn and co-host use a contemporary, upbeat format, sharing their successes and failures within their own families and talking about what the Lord is showing them. Visit www.oneplace.com to hear a new *Family Stuff* show from Dan Seaborn daily.

Winning At Home Moment—a one-minute Public Service Announcement (PSA) designed for secular radio. *Winning At Home Moment* offers thoughts that are simple, fun, challenging, concise, and practical. Every family can learn to have a winning home team.

Family Moments—a two-minute Christian radio program heard daily on over 500 stations across the country as well as overseas. *Family Moments* features many of Dan Seaborn's most popular illustrations, which entertain and challenge listeners.

Visit our website to find what *Winning At Home* **radio programs are aired in your area, and to see the complete line of Winning At Home resources.**

www.winningathome.com or call: 800-772-7202